Argument Evaluation

Stephen Naylor Thomas

Worthington Publishing Company
Tampa, Florida

Library of Congress Cataloging in Publication Data

Thomas, Stephen N. 1942-

      Argument Evaluation / Stephen Naylor Thomas
         p. 144   15 cm x 22.5 cm

         ISBN 0-9618359-1-5 : $9.95
         1. Reasoning.   2. Logic.   I. Title.
         BC177.T495   1991
         160--dc20   88-90262
                                          CIP

Cover by Rosell

Printed in the United States of America

10 9 8 7 6 5 4 3 2 1

ISBN 0-9618359-1-5
Library of Congress Catalog Card Number: 88-090262

Worthington Publishing Company
P.O. Box 16691
6907-202 Halifax River Drive
Tampa, FL 33687-6691

Available to textbook centers and retail bookstores from Baker &Taylor and other
fine wholesalers and distributors

Contents

Introduction

What is logic? Basically, logic is the study of the nature and characteristics of good reasoning, and the differences between good ("correct") and bad ("incorrect") reasoning. Ordinary language makes some of the same distinctions as logic. For example:

> Rational vs. Irrational
> Logical vs. Illogical
> Reasonable vs. Unreasonable
> Correct vs. Incorrect
> True vs. False
> Valid vs. Invalid
> Sound vs. Unsound

The last two pairs of terms have more exact technical meanings in logic, as will be seen in Chapter 1.

Good reasoning tends toward correct answers, accurate judgments, and best decisions. Bad reasoning cannot be relied upon to lead to correct answers, accurate judgments, and best decisions. Sound reasoning tends to lead only to conclusions that are true and that actually work in practice when applied to the real world. Unsound reasoning, in contrast, is more likely to end up with conclusions that are false or unreliable.

Why study logic? One reason for studying logic is its value for us in our own lives. Learning how to reason logically will help us to arrive at true conclusions and make the best decisions. There are, of course, other possible approaches. One can flip a coin, consult a fortune teller, or follow his or her instincts or impulses of the moment. This textbook does not tell you how to live your life. But if you would like to gain mastery of effective methods of thought, you will find the tools of logical reasoning here at your disposal. Whether or not you choose to use these methods, you can always be certain of their reliability.

Why do the methods of logic work? Not simply because logicians say that certain steps of reasoning are "correct." Rather, logicians try to discover and clarify the characteristics of reasoning that actually does tend to lead to correct

1

results. Logic follows facts. If a certain pattern of reasoning were discovered to be unreliable, logic would reject it.

Logic is not an enemy of feeling, emotion, or passion. If it is true, as the philosopher Pascal said, that "the heart has reasons of its own," logic can take these reasons into account and work with them too. Instead of opposing the heart's desires, logic can actually help the heart achieve its desires. Thus, for example, if I wanted to live as a mystic, or a hermit, or a shepherd, or in some nonrational state of consciousness, and if by sound logical reasoning, I concluded that this way of life would indeed really be best, then I could follow my chosen path with heart — reinforced by logical judgment!

Although logic and emotion do not automatically oppose each other, conflicts sometimes arise. Plato and other philosophers have pointed out that the human character contains many different inclinations that can run counter to each other, and that sometimes it is best for the rational mind to control and restrain passions or emotional impulses when they are contrary to everyone's best interests. It is easy, for example, to imagine circumstances in which I might desire to hit another person who is making me angry, but in which it might actually be in my own best interests (and more rational) not to do so, but to do something else instead. The same is true of many other impulses. So logic, right reason, and good judgment sometimes can be highly valuable in dealing with situations in which blind passion or emotional impulses might lead to actions contrary to our own good.

Also, although reason and emotion frequently agree with each other and logic often helps in reaching the heart's desires, situations can arise in which one wants to believe something when there is no justification for it and when, in fact, the belief would be false. In such cases, reason and emotion can oppose each other, and the use of logic is necessary if one wishes true knowledge rather than false belief.

Logic is highly valuable (and sometimes absolutely necessary) as a means of finding the truth not only in philosophical and theoretical reasoning generally, but often also in practical matters and daily commonplace concerns, including decision making. Actions taken after careful deliberation, using reason and logic, are usually actions that one is happiest about later on, whereas decisions made on a logically unsound basis often are regretted later. Logic can be used to find the true and correct answers to questions like "Is abortion right or wrong?," "Should our country be in its current military involvements?," "What am I doing, and what should I be doing, here in school?," and other important questions about economics, the environment, society, science, philosophy, and our personal lives. The ability to think logically and rationally is also an enormous help to you in getting a better job, advancing, and succeeding in whatever one does.

Someone may ask, "But what's the point of studying logic when other people are so illogical? Often you can't convince people with logical argument." Yes, it is sad but true that people sometimes are swayed by emotional appeal, flattery, advertising (including all the "hidden persuaders"), propaganda, and in extreme situations, by brainwashing, air raids, torture, and other forms of terrorism. But it is also true that sound logical arguments sometimes are highly useful in persuading people of truths that they did not formerly believe. Moreover, the beliefs produced by emotions often are variable and transitory, while a sound argument is objective and often produces beliefs that are permanent. Beliefs produced by sound arguments frequently are more firmly held and better defended than beliefs produced by nonlogical means.

But even if there existed other, more effective, ways of moving people than by showing them sound arguments, there still would be good reasons for studying logic. For the study of logic can help us distinguish truth from error in science, engineering, medicine, politics, economics, government, law, business, philosophy, and in our personal lives. Logic can help us to clarify our own thinking and writing, with far-reaching benefits for our lives. Logical thinking, unlike irrational thinking, gives us a more accurate idea of what we can expect from life, of our own shortcomings and abilities, of what we should pursue and what we should avoid, and of what strategies and tactics we should use to obtain the good, and to live well and be happy, thereby helping us to succeed in the great adventure and drama of living.[1] The strongest reason for studying logic probably is not for its use in winning arguments and convincing other people of the truth of our beliefs, but rather as a means of discovering for ourselves what the truth really is and how we should live.

Knowing the truth usually helps a person to live well and be happy. Thus, a primary reason for studying logic is the fact that it is in one's own personal best interests to do so. Logic is useful as means of gaining real knowledge and using it to live well and be happy.

There are also social and political reasons for encouraging others to study logic. In a society where voting citizens make crucial political choices that affect the lives and welfare of ALL the citizens (including ourselves), obviously it is in *everyone's* best interests (including our own) to educate as many citizens as possible to a level of rational thinking that will *minimize* the likelihood of their being led to false conclusions, incorrect judgments, and unwise decisions by propaganda, irrational emotional appeals, and bad logic, and that will *maximize* their chances of reaching correct conclusions and making the best decisions. For, if our fellow citizens are irrational in their thinking and actions, this is hazardous to us as well as to them (for example, the danger of nuclear war,

---

[1] The meaning of the phrase "live well" here goes beyond just material standards of living to include *everything* of value.

contamination or destruction of the environment, massive economic collapse, etc.). Illogical thinking can, and often does, lead people into disastrous actions that are contrary to everyone else's best interests and happiness, as well as their own. So it is wise to attempt to help other people raise the level of their rationality as much as possible. Rational thinkers will recognize that it is in their own best interests, when living in a democracy, for *everyone* to be capable of thinking rationally and reasoning logically. Consequently, when one sees someone having difficulty learning logic, one should not become impatient, resentful, or angry. *Even if* the situation were considered only from a purely selfish personal standpoint, with no social consciousness and no concern for other people's well being, one should try to help that person learn to reason logically with the best methods available. This is all the more true, obviously, when this education is viewed from the standpoint of a concern for the well being and happiness of other persons. The antiquated notion that the study of logic is suitable for only an elite group that claims to have "high mental horsepower" is philosophically shallow, thoughtless, and itself shows bad reasoning.

Logic and Language

Reasoning generally involves using language (with some nonverbal exceptions in painting, mechanics, geometry, and some instinctive, spontaneous behavior). Usually when people reason, their thinking involves language, whether they speak out loud or in a silent internal monologue. Because of the intimate relationship between reasoning and language, logic examines reasoning expressed in language. In particular, our study of logic will focus on certain important relationships between "reasons" and "conclusions" stated in the English language and we will learn to distinguish between logical and illogical combinations of statements. Although some knowledge of grammar is helpful, everything you need to know will be explained as we go along.

In the first chapter, you will acquire fundamental concepts and basic skills that will prepare you to apply logic. However, the details of the methods will be less important than the underlying abilities acquired, abilities that will serve you well for the rest of your life. Some of the detailed steps in the procedures in this textbook resemble the extra training wheels sometimes attached to beginners' bicycles: once the necessary skill has been mastered, they no longer need to be used, because correct judgments are made automatically.

Natural and Artificial Languages

This book focuses on reasoning in *natural languages*. A natural language is a symbol system that has developed historically as a means of communication.

English, French, German, Dutch, Spanish, Chinese, Swahili, and Hopi are examples of natural languages. An *artificial language,* on the other hand, is a language that was deliberately and intentionally constructed by a small group of thinkers to serve some special purpose. Computer languages, such as Fortran and Cobol, are examples of artificial languages; these languages, of course, are not spoken, but are used to write computer programs. During the past century, logicians and philosophers have developed a number of artificial *formal* languages that use symbolic and mathematical notation for the study of logic and other special purposes. They are not used for conversation. A typical sentence in one of these artificial languages looks more like a mathematical formula. For example: '$(x)(y)(Fxy)$'. (Translated into English, this formula reads: "For each entity, x, and each entity y, x stands in the relation F to y.") For the purposes of logic, a method based on an artificial language as contrasted with a natural language has both advantages and disadvantages. In this book we will enjoy the advantages of working with a natural language.

Two Traditional Approaches to Logic

Logic can be approached in different ways. Formal logic, one traditional approach, studies reasoning expressed in certain artificial languages. Some advocates of a formal approach believe that: (1) It is possible to translate any reasoning in a natural language into the symbols of an artificial formal language; (2) it is possible to evaluate precisely the corresponding formulae in the artificial language using certain mechanical procedures; and (3) the results of this evaluation can then be carried back to the original reasoning in natural language. Unfortunately, the required initial translation of natural-language sentences into the artificial language used in formal logic is, in many of the most important cases, at most, *possible only in principle,* as even the most enthusiastic advocates of formal logic now generally admit. In actual practice, the translations often turn out to be too difficult to make. Indeed, the philosopher Ludwig Wittgenstein (1889-1951), in his later writings, suggested that because of fundamental differences between natural and artificial formal languages, such translations are often not even possible in principle. Whether this criticism is correct or incorrect, many logicians now agree that the methods of formal logic are of little practical usefulness in dealing with most reasoning encountered in real-life situations. Another problem with formal logic is that the required artificial languages must be learned before its methods can be applied, and thus takes a long time because they are extremely complicated (like higher mathematics). These are some of the reasons why we will not take a formal approach. After studying this text, however, if you have the time and opportunity, and are interested, I certainly urge you to go on also to study formal (often called just "symbolic") logic — as well as the philosophy of logic — so that you can benefit from it, and judge for yourself its strengths and limitations.

Another traditional approach to logic is called the "informal fallacies" method. In this approach, samples are examined of various kinds of incorrect reasoning that commonly occur in natural languages. Students learn special names for each kind of mistake (for example, "the fallacy of arguing from ignorance") and are taught to recognize these specific kinds of errors and avoid them. One limitation to this approach is that the list of informal fallacies studied never covers more than a tiny percentage of all the different mistakes that occur in reasoning. Consequently, the informal-fallacies approach to logic provides no universally applicable way of distinguishing correct reasoning from incorrect reasoning.

The Advent of New Methods

The problems and difficulties with traditional approaches to logic led to the present development of a new method and underlying model for the direct analysis and evaluation of reasoning as it actually occurs in a natural language (here, English). It is called "Direct Logic®." No translation into any artificial language is required in this new method, and both the language talked about (the *object language*) and the language used for this talk (the *metalanguage*) are natural.

Do not confuse *natural language* with *ordinary* (or *everyday*) language. Highly advanced, complex theoretical statements can be made in natural language. In fact, specialized scientific, philosophic, and other technical statements are made in natural languages far more often than in an artificial language. Consequently, my methods will work well not only on ordinary everyday reasoning, but also on all theoretical, technical, legal, political, economic, scientific, or philosophic reasoning. For the same reason, they also will help in your readings, discussions, papers, and exams in other subjects.

Thinkers have used Direct Natural Logic® successfully to figure out, for example, how to:

> evaluate career plans and achieve professional success
> solve major intellectual and theoretical problems in the arts and
>   sciences
> finance college educations for their children
> "live like millionaires" without being millionaires
> make fortunes without getting out of their easy chair
> resolve close personal and family conflicts and problems
> locate and meet a suitable mate for themselves, even from a distance

escape impending catastrophes that will destroy the irrational people
around them

solve serious medical, financial, and other personal problems that had
confounded doctors and other expert authorities

cure otherwise unsolvable mental and emotional problems in
themselves and others

find a good job that they enjoy

set up and manage organizations and business ventures, making them
flourish

repair and improve machinery, motor vehicles, computers, home-
entertainment systems, and other material conveniences

answer satisfactorily fundamental ethical, religious, and philosophic
questions

make complex decisions logically, selecting the best of the competing
options in a way that will stand the test of time

prosper even during times of economic downturn

recognize important, and even potentially disastrous, errors in
information others presented to them for their action

escape war, eliminate boredom, minimize taxes legally, avoid or win
lawsuits

detect unwise investment proposals, fraudulent financial offers, and
bad plans

live well and be happy

Many animals (including some members of our species) get along without logic, but when logic is needed, the outcome may be life-or-death.

Please understand that Direct Logic® does not show one how to do all these things in a mechanical way, like a cookbook. That probably is impossible. Instead, it gives one the thinking skills to figure all this out for oneself, as the need arises, in the particular circumstances in which one finds oneself. The only other thing needed, besides mastery of logical thinking skills (and other information you acquired through education) are the habits of mind and character traits of a good critical thinker. There have been people who were good at logic only in an academic setting, but lacked the mental habits and character traits that are also necessary to put logic to work for them in their lives.[1] Without putting logical thinking skills into practice, the full benefits of logic are not enjoyed.

Another important advantage of the methods and concepts of Direct Natural Logic® is that they apply not only to natural languages, but also to the

---

[1] It has been rumored that there are even some teachers of logic and critical thinking who do not think critically about their subject.

artificial languages used in formal symbolic logic. So, if you later decide to take another course based on a formal-logic approach, your previous study of Direct Logic® will help you.

Whatever your long-range reasons for studying logic, this textbook will help you to sharpen your own thinking and reasoning, and understand and evaluate critically more accurately and profoundly what you read and hear. Exercises follow each section of text. It is important to complete and review these exercises before going on to the next section.

If you like what you learn from this brief mini-text, and see a potential value for yourself in further developing your logical skills along these lines, you may wish to enroll in a course using one of the other textbooks listed on the back cover. Enjoy the book.

1
When is Reasoning Reliable?

In trying to prove or explain something by means of reasoning, one or more statements called "reasons" or "premises" are given as justifying, supporting, or explaining some "conclusion(s)." In the simplest case, this situation is diagrammed as follows:

Reason(s)

Conclusion

The arrow in this diagram can be read as the word "therefore." It represents the *step of reasoning,* or "inference" from the reason(s) to the conclusion. Here is an example:

It is impossible to beat the house
at gambling.

You cannot beat the house at gambling.

This diagram pictures the reasoning. When a diagram, or picture, like this is presented, it does not necessarily mean that one agrees with the reasoning or thinks that it is any good. One may think that there is something wrong with the reasoning, or that it is "unsound." In that case, the diagram is a picture of some reasoning that one thinks is unsound. The diagram then is a way of displaying the reasoning that one thinks is unsound, a way of showing someone else what reasoning one is talking about. Of course, it is also possible that one may believe the reasoning to be good (or "sound" as logicians call good reasoning). Finally, it is possible that one may be *uncertain* whether the reasoning is sound or unsound, and in this case, the diagram may function as a useful tool, because by studying it carefully, one may be able to determine whether the reasoning is sound or unsound. Here is an example:

The term "God," by definition, is the
name of a necessarily existing Being.

↓

It is false by definition to say that God
does not exist.

Many attempted proofs and disproofs that one encounters are in this third category: at first, it is not immediately obvious whether they are sound or unsound, but by examining a diagram of the reasoning, eventually it is possible to determine whether they are sound or unsound.

Reasoning is sound if it successfully proves or explains its conclusion. Reasoning is unsound if it fails to prove or explain its conclusion. This book shows how to tell whether any given reasoning is reliable or unreliable — that is, sound or unsound.

When two or more reasons, or premises, need to be combined together to support a conclusion, they are diagrammed as linked together by a "+" symbol, with a horizontal underline also connecting them, like this:

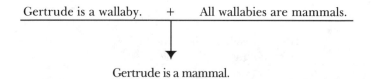

Gertrude is a wallaby.   +   All wallabies are mammals.

↓

Gertrude is a mammal.

Several reasons can also support the same conclusion in separate, independent ways, and when this happens, instead of being linked together in the diagram, they will be diagrammed as "converging" separately on the same conclusion, as shown in the next diagram:

Soaking potted plants in the
sink or tub waters the soil
completely, through and
through.

Soaking potted plants in the
sink or tub washes out excess
fertilizer salts that may have
accumulated.

It is good to soak potted plants in the sink or tub occasionally.

With interesting arguments, however, usually several reasons are combined or linked together to support the conclusion.

In any given diagram, some reasons will appear at the top with no arrows above them. These are called the argument's **"basic reasons."** They are the ultimate premises or assumptions on which the reasoning is based. In the wallaby example, the statements "Gertrude is a wallaby" and "All wallabies are mammals" are two basic reasons.

Long, complicated arguments may involve several steps of reasoning, or "inferences," coming one after another. For example, the following famous attempted proof of the existence of God has two steps of reasoning, each of which is represented by one arrow:

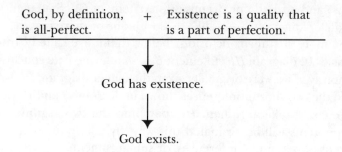

In the philosophy of religion, one might try to figure out whether this argument is sound. Right now, it is only being used as a simple example of reasoning containing more than one step of inference and diagrammed with more than one arrow.

Arguments with several inferences are evaluated as if they were several one-step arguments connected together, one after another. To understand this, let us begin by imagining that we have two arguments, one going from statement A, as a reason or premise, to statement B, as a conclusion, and a second argument going from the same statement B, now functioning as a basic reason or premise (in the second argument), to statement C as a conclusion:

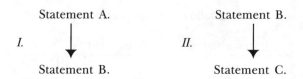

Since the same statement B that appears as a conclusion of the first argument also appears as a premise or reason in the second argument, we can, if we want, put the two short arguments together to make a longer argument, containing two steps of inference, as follows:

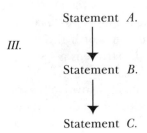

Notice that statement *B* in diagram *III* is shown as both a conclusion (from statement *A*) and a reason or premise (for statement *C*). Statements that come in the middle of longer diagrams like this, with one or more reasons above them, and one or more further conclusions below them, are called **"intermediate conclusions."** In diagram *III*, statement *B* is an intermediate conclusion.

Obviously, if we were originally given the longer diagram, *III*, we could take it apart into the two shorter inferences shown in diagrams *I* and *II*, each with one arrow. We could take argument *III* apart into the two arguments, *I* and *II*. Longer arguments will be evaluated this way, by taking them apart into their separate steps of reasoning, inferences, or sub-arguments.

The same can also be done when some, or all, of the steps of inference involve several reasons linked together. For example, suppose that a complex argument looked like this

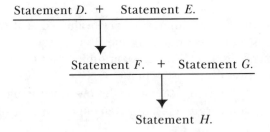

This can be taken apart into the following two component steps of reasoning:

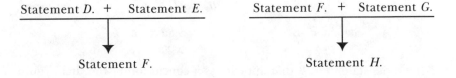

To break an argument down like this, proceed as follows: For each separate arrow in the original big diagram, find the statement or statements immediately above it and the statement immediately below it and separate these from the rest of the original argument, recopying just this part of the diagram separately.

In fact, you do not even need to recopy or make new separate diagrams: with practice, you can develop the ability to focus your attention on each step of inference separately, lifting it out of the context of the larger argument simply in your mind. For practice, try to take the last example of an attempted proof of the existence of God apart mentally, looking first at the part enclosed in the larger rectangle in the next figure and then at the part enclosed in the smaller rectangle; look at the next diagram, and try to see the two subarguments, or separate steps of inference in it.

Original argument in discourse form:

> God, by definition, is all-perfect. Existence is a quality that is a part of perfection. Therefore, God has existence. From this it follows that God exists.
>
> — One version of the "Ontological Argument" for the existence of God.

Diagram Showing One Two-Step Argument:

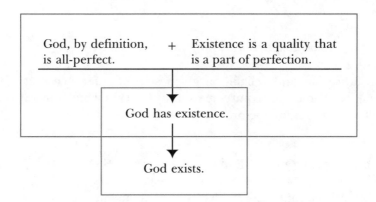

Try to imagine how the inferences in the two boxes could be set forth separately. When you think you see it, turn to the next figure to check your result.

This argument can be disassembled into two one-step arguments as follows:

Disassembled into two one-step arguments:

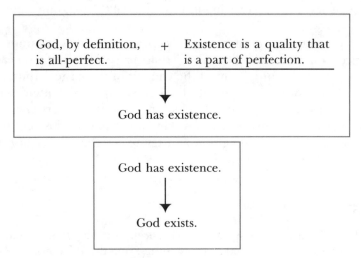

These two diagrams show the original argument pulled apart into two separate inferences or sub-arguments. Any long argument can be evaluated by taking it apart into separate steps of inference, and evaluating each step separately, one after another. For a long argument to be sound, each individual step of reasoning it contains must be sound. Like a chain, a proof is no stronger than its weakest link.

Two Requirements for Soundness and Reliability

To be sound and reliable, a given step of inference must fulfill two requirements. These two requirements, fully explained and illustrated at length in the following pages, can be preliminarily summarized as follows:

TWO REQUIREMENTS FOR SOUNDNESS

1. All relevant reasons (that is, the statements immediately above the arrow) are true.

2. The conclusion (the statement immediately below the arrow) follows logically from these reasons.

Thus, in order to know that we can rely on a piece of reasoning as sound, we need to know (1) that all relevant reasons are true, and (2) that the conclusion follows logically from those reasons. Do not worry if you do not yet fully understand this. Everything will be explained completely in the following pages.

1. Truth of Reasons

You probably already understand the meaning of the first requirement. A statement is "true" if it fits the facts (that is, corresponds to reality) and works in practice. If a statement fails to correspond to reality — that is, if it claims that the world is otherwise than it really is — then the statement is not true, but "false."

A statement is not, in general, made "true" just by someone saying it is true; it must actually correspond to the facts. If a person believes that a statement is true when actually it is false, or if a person believes a statement to be false when actually it is true, then that person is mistaken.

When one is given a statement, one might know that it definitely is true, or one might know that it definitely is false, or one might not know or be uncertain.[1] Perhaps one can say with confidence that it is "probably true," or that it is "probably false," or one might not even know this much, and so one might need to say that one does not even know whether the statement is probably true or probably false. As part of evaluating reasoning, we will put each given reason into one of the following five categories:

CATEGORY	IS SHORT FOR:	EXAMPLE
Definitely true =	I know for a fact, with certainty, that this statement is true.	"Some roses are red."
Probably true =	It is highly likely that this statement is true, but I do not know this with complete certainty.	"All pure water under standard conditions boils at 100 degrees C."
Uncertain or Don't know =	I am uncertain, or do not know, whether this statement is true or false.	"Killer bees will be able to survive above the frost belt."

---

[1] *Note to Advanced Readers:* The complete method presented here naturally integrates logical with epistemic considerations.

Probably false   =   It is highly likely that   "I can run a mile in six
                       this statement is false,   minutes."
                       but I do not know this
                       with complete certainty.

Definitely false   =   I know for a fact, with   "All ducks are black."
                       certainty, that this
                       statement is false.

These ratings can vary from person to person. A statement that I correctly categorize as a "Don't know" might be correctly categorized as "Definitely true" by someone else who has access to information unavailable to me. Of course, a statement cannot be both "true" and "false," because if it is false, then it is not true. If person X says that a statement is "definitely true," and person Y says that it is "definitely false," for example, then at least one of these two persons must be mistaken.

Also, the truth or falsity of statements made by sentences containing pronouns (like "I" or "that") depend on who or what is denoted by the pronoun(s); with one reference, it may be a true statement, and with another reference it may be a false statement. For example, the words, "I can run a mile in six minutes" probably express a false statement if the pronoun "I" refers to me (because I am a poor runner), but they could express a true statement if uttered by a person who is a good runner. Different statements are made when pronouns change reference, so one statement can be true, while another can be false.

In order for a step of reasoning to be sound and reliable, all relevant reasons directly above the arrow in its diagram must receive a rating of "Definitely true," or at least, "Probably true." Consider, for example, the following reasoning:

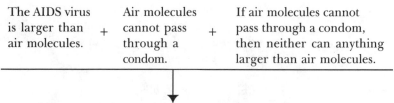

The AIDS virus   Air molecules   If air molecules cannot
is larger than   +   cannot pass   +   pass through a condom,
air molecules.   through a   then neither can anything
                      condom.   larger than air molecules.

The AIDS virus cannot pass through a condom.

In order to rely on this reasoning with complete confidence, one would need to know at minimum that each of the three reasons is, at least, probably true.

Of course, there can be reasoning that is actually (unknown to me) objectively sound, but that I am unable to accept with confidence, or rely on, because I do not *know* that all the reasons are true (even though, unknown to me, they are actually true). In such cases, one may need additional reasoning that starts from *other premises* that one *knows* to be true in order to establish the truth of the crucial reasons that one did not previously know to be true.

If some of the relevant reasons are definitely false statements, then one can discard as unsound the part of the reasoning that involves them, because it fails the first requirement that all relevant reasons be true. It should be clearly understood, at all times, that categorizing reasoning as "unsound" does not mean that its conclusion is false. Unsound arguments can be given for conclusions that are, in fact, true. To call an argument "unsound" only means that the reasoning fails to justify its conclusion. Here is a simple example of unsound reasoning that happens to have a true conclusion:

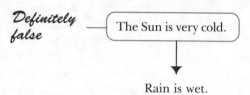

Rain is wet.

This reasoning is unsound, due, among other problems, to a definitely false reason. But the conclusion is true. As this example illustrates, the fact that reasoning is unsound does not mean that the conclusion (here, "Rain is wet") is false. (If it did, then you could prove the *falsity* of any true statement by simply constructing some dumb unsound argument in favor of it.) For an argument to be unsound simply means that it fails to prove the truth of its conclusion; its conclusion can still be true, and there may even be some other sound argument that proves it. In geometry class, for example, one student's unsound reasoning may fail to prove a theorem that another student is able to deduce flawlessly with a different line of reasoning that *is* sound.

As part of evaluating the soundness of inferences, we will attempt to judge accurately the truth or falsity of the reason(s) above the arrow. These evaluations can be recorded by circling or "lassoing" each reason separately, and writing one of the five ratings distinguished earlier at the other end of the lasso. Notice that although in tests in other subjects in school, the answer "I don't know" may receive no credit, saying "I don't know" or "I am uncertain" may be exactly the correct response in what we are doing here (and in philosophy as well as life generally). Also, some difficult cases will arise later where we will have to clarify the statements given as reasons before we can even give one of these ratings (due, for example, to their extreme unclarity), but you will be shown how to handle this problem then. Remember that evaluating the truth or falsity of the reasons is only one of the two steps required to evaluate soundness, and that the second step has not yet been discussed or explained.

Here, for example, is my evaluation of the *truth or falsity of the reasons* in the earlier example about the wallaby:

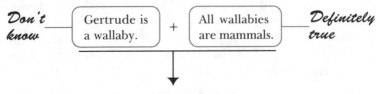

Gertrude is a mammal.

I put "Don't know" beside "Gertrude is a wallaby," because I do not even know to whom (or what) the term "Gertrude" refers; if you happened to know what this word names (perhaps a certain animal in an Australian zoo?), then you might be in a position to give a different rating (perhaps "Definitely true" or "Definitely false"). Similarly, with reference to the other reason, people who know nothing about wallabies might have to write "Don't know" beside "All wallabies are mammals," because they do not know whether wallabies are mammals. What appears beside the lassos around the statements in the diagram is my evaluation based on what I do and do not know. Your ratings might be different (although if someone rated "All wallabies are mammals" as "Definitely false," that person would be mistaken). Since I do not know whether one of the reasons in the wallaby example is true, it is unknown to me whether this reasoning passes the first test (unless I meet Gertrude). I do not know whether it is sound or not. It might be sound, but if it is, I do not know this, because I do not know whether all the relevant reasons are true. I might say, "I shall put it on the back burner until I find out," except that probably most reasoning that one encounters in life will go into this "Can't say" category, so the metaphorical back burner will not be large enough to hold it all, and I'll probably just end up tossing this example in the waste basket.

The word "relevant" in the formulation of the first requirement for reasoning to be sound (namely, "All *relevant* reasons are true") allows for the unusual case in which one or more extraneous or irrelevant statements are included (for example, as a joke, or by mistake) among the reasons above the arrow. In cases where a sound argument can be produced by cutting out some irrelevant reason(s) from the diagram, we may do so, and even say that the original argument (as fixed up) was basically sound.

2. Validity of the Step(s) of Inference

Besides having true reasons, the other requirement that reasoning must fulfill in order to be sound is that the conclusion must *follow logically* from the reason(s). Logicians use the word "**valid**" with a special technical meaning to describe reasoning in which the conclusion really does follow logically from the reason(s). Being *valid* is a second requirement that must be met by reasoning in order to prove or explain its conclusion. Reasoning that fails to pass this requirement because the conclusion does not follow logically from the reasons is said to be "invalid." Thus, reasoning in which the conclusion really does follow logically is said to be "valid," and reasoning in which the conclusion fails to follow logically from the reasons is said to be "invalid." These two terms are used in logic in a special technical sense that is different from their loose meaning in ordinary everyday language. The special technical meaning of the terms "valid" and "invalid" in logic will now be explained in more detail. Later in this chapter, we will separate two degrees of "validity" ("deductively valid" and "strong") from three degrees of "invalidity" ("moderate," "weak," and "nil"), but for now let us just begin with the distinction between valid and invalid.

Whether reasoning is valid or invalid depends on the *logical relationship* of the conclusion to the reason(s). That is, whether a conclusion follows logically from given reasons depends on the relationship that exists between it and the statement(s) immediately above the arrow in the diagram. The relationship that needs to exist in order for the conclusion to follow logically from the reasons is this: the conclusion needs to be related to the reason(s) in such a way that *the truth of the reasons, if they were true, would make it highly unlikely or impossible for the conclusion to be false.* [1] If the statements below and above the arrow are related to each other in this way, then the reasoning is "valid"; if this relationship does not exist, then the reasoning is "invalid." The following is an example of reasoning that meets the validity requirement:

It is impossible to beat the house at gambling.

You cannot beat the house at gambling.

This inference passes the validity test because, necessarily, IF the statement given above the arrow as a reason be true, then this fact would guarantee the

---

[1]*Note to Advanced Readers:* Readers previously acquainted with formal deductive logic are forewarned that the application of the term "valid" as used in direct logic is NOT restricted to formally valid arguments, or even to deductively valid arguments. "Inductive reasoning" will also be counted "valid" if it establishes its conclusion beyond a reasonable doubt. In natural language, *failure* to be formally valid, or even deductively valid, does not automatically entail that reasoning is "invalid."

truth of the statement given as a conclusion. In other words, if the statement "It is impossible to beat the house at gambling" be true, then the statement "You cannot beat the house at gambling" must also be true; that is, the statement given as a conclusion cannot fail to be true IF the statement given as a reason be true.[1]

If, on the other hand, an inference is such that the truth of the given reason(s) would *not* guarantee the truth of the drawn conclusion, then the conclusion does not follow logically from these reasons, and the reasoning is invalid. Here is an obvious example:

The Sun is very hot.

↓ *(invalid*

London is the capital of England.

Although both the reason and the conclusion appearing in this diagram are true statements, this reasoning is invalid (which means that the conclusion does not follow logically from the premise), because the truth of the premise does nothing to make the truth of the conclusion likely. This is shown by the fact that it is easy to imagine the reason being true and yet the conclusion being false. I can

---

[1]*Note to Advanced Readers: Objection:* "You seem oblivious to the need to state a piece of reasoning in a reasonable complete way before evaluating it. This reasoning is not valid unless it is understood to incorporate the unstated premise 'You cannot do anything that it is impossible to do.' If, as you state, 'The validity of the reasoning depends only on the logical relationships among the statements in the diagram,' then this argument is deductively invalid." *Reply:* In evaluating reasoning, we take it as given that the symbols in the arguments carry the meanings they have in the language being used, whether that language be artificial or natural. Given these meanings, the inference is valid as it stands, because the statement "You cannot do anything that it is impossible to do" is true by definition, true analytically, given the semantics or meanings of the terms. Thus, as it stands, the inference is a deductively valid semantic entailment. If one likes, when evaluating an inference using these methods, one can consider the totality of analytic and semantic truths to be automatically added to the given reasons. Only if they are contingent (synthetic) statements must collateral assumptions be explicitly stated.

If the objector were asked why he did not think it necessary also to add to his premise another (third) premise stating, "If it is impossible to beat the house at gambling and you cannot do anything that it is impossible to do, then you cannot beat the house at gambling," presumably he would say that this does not need to be stated explicitly because its truth is already given implicitly by the definitions of the terms involved ("if," "then," "and," etc.), and that the original conclusion follows directly from the *two* premises he gave when these terms are understood to have their normal semantics or meaning. Direct logic gives the same reason to explain why the additional premise he proposed was not needed either.

Of course, in saying that all relevant analytic truths in the natural language can, if one likes, be imagined added as unstated premises to each inference as it is evaluated, it must be remembered, as Quine notes, that the totality of truths cannot be sharply divided into two mutually exclusive subsets, the "analytic truths" vs. the "synthetic truths," since no statement is immune to revision, not even the "necessary truths" or "logical truths" of formal logic. This fact will ultimately mean that the line between "deductively valid" and "strong" inferences in natural language is not completely sharp, and that it too is a difference of degree, a fact well-accommodated by direct logic.

easily imagine that the statement "The Sun is very hot" is true while at the same time imagining that some other city (say, Oxford) is the capital of England. Because of this genuine possibility, this conclusion does not follow logically from this reason. In other words, this reasoning is invalid because it is a real possibility that the conclusion could be false even though the reason given is true. A step of reasoning is invalid whenever falsity of the conclusion remains a genuine possibility even when the reason(s) be assumed true. The mere existence of such a *genuine possibility* is enough to make an inference invalid. For reasoning to be valid, any such possibility must be eliminated by the form or content of the statement(s) given as reason(s). The previous example about gambling met this requirement for validity.

Reasoning that is invalid is said to be a **"non sequitur,"** which means in Latin, "it does not follow."

Notice two important facts about validity, as illustrated by these examples. (1) The validity of reasoning only depends on the logical relationships among the statements in the diagram. Validity primarily depends on what is inside, or internal to, the diagram as written.[1] Validity is a matter of the *relationship between the strings of words above and below the arrow.* Thus, we can usually determine whether or not reasoning is valid simply by examining these symbols and thinking about their meaning. (2) The statements in the diagram do not need actually to be true in order for the reasoning to be valid. Reasoning can be valid even if some or all of the statements involved are false. This is because validity only requires that the statements be *related to each other* in such a way that it would be unlikely or impossible for the conclusion to be false IF the reason(s) were true. It does not require that the reasons actually be true. For example, the following inference is valid, even though the statement given as a reason is definitely false:

No cats are pets.

↓ *(valid)*

No pets are cats.

I know that the premise is false, because I know of some cats that are pets. But the conclusion follows validly from this false premise, because if it were true that "No cats are pets," then it would have to be true that "No pets are cats." So, it is possible to reason validly from false premises or from false assumptions, as in this example. Indeed, this occurs frequently.

---

[1]Sometimes, however, in real cases in natural language, certain additional "understood" statements are treated as if they were added to the reasons, as will be seen later.

Validity only requires that the reason(s) be related to the conclusion in such a way that the truth of the reason(s), IF the reason(s) were true, would make the truth of the conclusion at least highly likely. Remember that in order to be SOUND — that is, in order to prove or explain its conclusion — reasoning also must have true reasons. But it need not have true reasons in order to be *valid*. The need for correspondence to reality is taken care of by the first requirement (that all the relevant reasons be true). The second requirement (that the reasoning be valid) makes a further demand. Reasoning with false reasons fails the first requirement for soundness, but it can still be valid. Of all the facts of logic, this is perhaps the most difficult for beginners to understand initially.

Here is another example of reasoning that is valid even though it has a false reason:

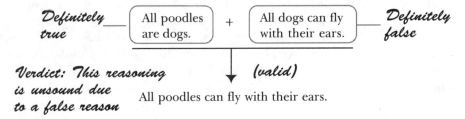

This reasoning is valid because the reasons are related to the conclusion in such a way that IF the reasons were true, their truth would make the truth of the conclusion highly likely or absolutely certain. One way to test my evaluation of its validity is by *imagining* that both reasons were true, and then seeing whether you can at the same time imagine any way in which the conclusion could be false. You will find that there is not. If you imagine a world in which all poodles are dogs and all dogs can fly with their ears, you are forced to imagine that in such a fantastic world, all poodles can fly with their ears too. So the reasoning is valid. But this reasoning is unsound, of course, due to the fact that one of the reasons is false, so it fails to prove its fantastic conclusion. I have indicated this by writing evaluations alongside the relevant parts of the diagram, as you will do on the exercises later.

The *validity* of any inference can be judged by starting with the following **magic question:** Is there any possible way in which the conclusion could be false even if (or even though) the reason(s) be true? An alternative version of the same question is to ask whether it is possible to conceive of a world in which the premises be true, and yet the conclusion be false. If the answer to this question is "No," then the inference is "valid." If the answer is "Yes," then next we ask the question: How likely or probable is the most likely of these possibilities? If every such possible way is highly unlikely, the inference still rates as "valid." But if one or more of these imaginable ways in which the conclusion could be false even if the reason(s) were true is a real possibility — a situation of the sort that has a genuine possibility or likelihood of arising in the real world — then the inference rates as "invalid."

Remember that reasoning is *unsound* whenever it fails to meet either the requirement of having true reasons, or the requirement of having valid reasoning (or fails both requirements). Here are additional examples:

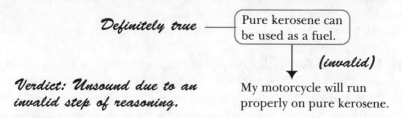

Definitely true ——— Pure kerosene can be used as a fuel.

(invalid)

Verdict: Unsound due to an invalid step of reasoning.   My motorcycle will run properly on pure kerosene.

It is true that kerosene is a fuel, but by itself, this does not *prove* that my motorcycle will run properly on kerosene. This is shown by the fact that it is quite possible for it to be true that "Kerosene is a fuel" while being false that my motorcycle will run properly on kerosene. It is conceivable, for example, that kerosene will work as a fuel in certain stoves and lamps, and yet that my motorcycle will not run properly on kerosene. The existence of this real possibility shows that the reasoning is invalid. Because the step of reasoning is invalid, the reasoning is unsound, despite the truth of the premise.

The opposite defect exists in the next example:

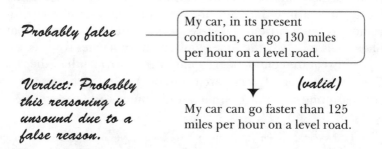

Probably false ——— My car, in its present condition, can go 130 miles per hour on a level road.

Verdict: Probably this reasoning is unsound due to a false reason.   *(valid)*

My car can go faster than 125 miles per hour on a level road.

From the standpoint of what I know about my car, I would classify the statement "My car, in its present condition, can go 130 mph on a level road" as probably false. But the reasoning is valid; the conclusion does follow logically from this false premise.[1] If I suppose it to be true that "My car, in its present condition,

---

[1]*Note to Advanced Readers:* At this point, the following *objection* may be raised: "This reasoning is invalid as diagrammed, i.e., without the added premise that 130 mph is faster than 125 mph. This may seem a picky

can go 130 mph on a level road," then there is no way that I can escape also imagining that it can go faster than 125 mph, so the conclusion does follow logically from this false premise. But since the premise is false, the argument is unsound.

Someone may object:

"Why permit arguments with false reasons ever to be considered 'valid'? We know that arguments with false reasons are unsound and unreliable. It seems strange to allow that some arguments with false premises can still be 'valid'."

Reply: There are several good reasons for recognizing that reasoning with false premises can still be "valid."

(1) First, according to the given definition of "valid," as it was formulated, an argument that has false reasons can still be "valid." The two requirements of *(i)* truth of reasons and *(ii)* validity of inference are separate conditions that are independent of each other. When two separate conditions for something exist, to think that one requirement must, in that case, be identical to the other is a confusion. A simple example of an analogous situation is the following. In order to vote in an election in many countries, these two requirements must be satisfied: a person must be a citizen of the country, and also, the person must have reached the legal voting age. Notice that either of these requirements can be satisfied without satisfying the other. For example, a person could be a citizen, but not yet be old enough to vote. Or, a person could be of legal voting age, and yet not be a citizen. Obviously it would be a great confusion to think that because someone did not meet the first requirement of citizenship, therefore this person did not meet the second requirement of age either — or to think that because a little boy did not meet the age requirement for voting, therefore he was not a citizen. Likewise, it is a confusion to think that because an argument fails to satisfy the first requirement of having true reasons, it also fails the second requirement of being valid. Because *(i)* truth of the reasons and *(ii)* validity of the step of inference are two separate, independent requirements, a piece of reasoning can meet either requirement without also meeting the

objection given the obviousness of what is missing in this example, but students need to be taught to make necessary assumptions explicit. Not to do this invites credulity in the face of arguments having less obvious premises which are deliberately left unstated because they express prejudices or other beliefs that will not withstand examination." *Reply:* Some traditional logicians may insist that such inferences become deductively valid only when we add certain "hidden premises" like this. But if we evaluate the original inference just as it stands, we will find that as it stands, it is deductively valid, not invalid. If the given premise is true, then the conclusion must (in the strongest sense of "must") also be true. If an argument is missing a premise that is not a necessary or analytic truth but rather a "prejudice or other belief that will not withstand examination," we will rate the reasoning as invalid, or else require that this premise be made explicit and then critically consider whether it is true, using the methods in this text.

other. In particular, an argument can satisfy the requirement of being valid, while failing the requirement of having true reasons. (The earlier poodle example, and the cats example, already illustrated this.)

(2) A second reason for recognizing that reasoning with false premises still can be valid is that doing so permits a further use for logic: in addition to using reasoning to discover and prove true conclusions, it also enables us to use logic to discover and refute false assumptions and mistaken beliefs, in a way that we could not use unless we recognized that a conclusion can follow validly from false reasons. Recognizing this enables us to refute a controversial false statement by showing that another *known falsehood* can be validly inferred from it. Here is how this works. Suppose that the relationship between a premise and a conclusion is such that if the premise be true, then the conclusion would have to be true too, so that the reasoning is "valid." In that case, discovering that the *conclusion* happens to be, in fact, *false* would conclusively prove that the *premise also is false*. (If you do not at first understand this, stop and reflect on it for a moment until you do.) This enables erroneous statements to be proven false and conclusively refuted by showing that if they are assumed as premises, then a false conclusion validly follows from them. Thus, a correct understanding of the concept of validity gives us a way of refuting falsehoods as well as proving truths.

Here is a simple example. Some people oppose making contraceptives and birth control information available to teenagers on the grounds that these people wish to prevent teenagers from having sex at all, and they believe that preventing teenagers from having access to birth control devices and information will prevent teenagers from having sex. This belief might be proven false by showing that a false conclusion follows logically (that is, "validly") from it as the following example illustrates:

> I will show that it is mistaken to think that if teenagers have no birth control devices, they will not have sexual intercourse. Suppose that the assumption or claim in question were true. That is, suppose it were true that "If teenagers have no birth control devices, then they will not have sexual intercourse." Now obviously, if teenagers do not have sex, then there will be few, if any, teenage pregnancies. Therefore, from these two statements combined together, it follows logically that if teenagers have no birth control devices, then there will be few, if any, teenage pregnancies. This logically entails the further conclusion that teenagers having no birth control devices will seldom, if ever, become pregnant. But we know that this conclusion is false, since there are many teenage pregnancies every year. So, one of the two initial assumptions must be false. The second assumption, that is, "If teenagers do not have sex, there will be few, if any, teenage pregnancies," is beyond doubt, as a fact of biology, so the false assumption must be the other one. This proves that it is false to say

that "If teenagers have no birth control devices, then they will not have sex."

The reasoning in this example is so simple and straightforward as to be fairly obvious, but other, more complicated cases involving the same basic logical principles are less obvious, so let us diagram and study this simple example to make certain that we understand the logical principles involved, and the crucial role played by the concept of validity. In the diagram below of the preceding reasoning, notice how the false conclusion is drawn from premises that include the questionable assumption:

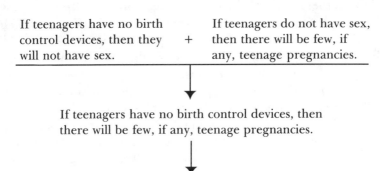

If teenagers have no birth   If teenagers do not have sex,
control devices, then they   +   then there will be few, if
will not have sex.   any, teenage pregnancies.

If teenagers have no birth control devices, then
there will be few, if any, teenage pregnancies.

Teenagers having no birth control devices
will seldom, if ever, become pregnant.

The fact that the *false final conclusion* at the bottom follows with deductive validity (in each step of inference) from the two basic assumptions at the top of the diagram *proves* that one (or more) of those two basic assumptions must also be false. If the assumptions were true, then so too would be the conclusion, because the reasoning is valid. So, since the conclusion is false, we can conclude that at least one of the two assumptions that logically entails this conclusion is false. We know independently that the assumption on the top right is true. Therefore, the top left assumption must be false.

As in this example, so too in general, false statements sometimes can be refuted like this by showing that they logically imply a false conclusion. This way of detecting and refuting *false* statements would be impossible if it were not recognized that reasoning with false premises can still be valid. This is a second reason for appreciating that reasoning with false premises can still be valid and that conclusions can follow logically from false assumptions. The reasoning is valid whenever the reason(s) and conclusion are related to each other in such a way that the truth of the reason(s) IF TRUE, WOULD make absolutely certain, or at least highly likely, the truth of the conclusion. In reasoning from false assumptions, we use our imagination to suppose, or pretend, that the reason(s) be true, and then determine whether, in that case the conclusion still could be false. If the answer is, "No, the conclusion could not be false if the reasons be true," then the reasoning is *"valid,"* even if one or more of the reasons is, in fact, false.

The process of drawing conclusions from false assumptions is used in the sciences, law, philosophy, and many other advanced disciplines to refute erroneous theories or principles by showing that a false or unacceptable consequence or prediction follows logically from them as a conclusion. If we failed to appreciate that a conclusion can follow logically, by valid inference, from false premises, this would be impossible. We could not use logic to discover errors and expose mistakes like this if the logical relationship of "validity" were not defined in such a way that it can exist between false assumptions and conclusions that follow logically from these false assumptions. Anyone who mistakenly thought that the falseness of assumptions automatically makes reasoning be invalid would be deprived of this important use for logic, and probably would always be confused in life too.

In the 130 mile-per-hour example, the unsound (but valid) reasoning had a conclusion that is probably false. But unsound reasoning can "luck out" and have a true conclusion too. Here is an example:

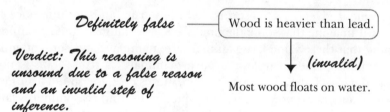

The statement given as the reason is definitely false, and the step of inference also is invalid (because one can easily imagine a conceivable world in which "Wood is heavier than lead" is true, but "Most wood floats on water" is false). Just imagine a world in which wood is heavier than lead and sinks in water. So, the truth of the statement given as the reason would not guarantee the truth of the statement given as the conclusion, and therefore the reasoning is invalid. Although the conclusion "Most wood floats on water" happens to be true, this reasoning fails to prove or explain this fact because it fails both requirements: the reason given is false and the step of inference is invalid. Sometimes unsound reasoning has a true conclusion, and sometimes it has a false conclusion. So the fact that reasoning is *unsound* does not, by itself, tell us anything about whether the conclusion is true or false.

But what about reasoning that is *sound*? If reasoning is sound, what does this tell us about the truth or falsity of its conclusion? Let's think about this very carefully to figure it out. First, let us remember that a sound inference meets both the requirement of having true reasons, and also the requirement of being valid. And as just explained, validity means that if the reason(s) be true, then it is at least highly likely that the conclusion is true too. So, in the case described, (1) the reasons are true, and (2) if the reasons are true, then the truth of the conclusion is highly likely. Thus, when both requirements for soundness are satisfied, the truth of the conclusion is at least highly likely. So, if we did not previously know that its conclusion is true, sound reasoning gives us the new knowledge that its conclusion is true. Since new knowledge is often useful and valuable, and may also enable us to find and correct errors in previous beliefs, and so, live well and be happy, sound reasoning obviously can give us something that is useful and valuable.

Of course, sound reasoning may have as its conclusion something that we already knew to be true. For example,

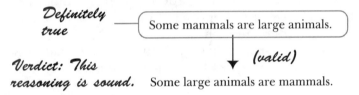

Definitely true

Some mammals are large animals.

Verdict: This reasoning is sound.   *(valid)*

Some large animals are mammals.

The statement given as a reason is definitely true, and the inference is valid because if I imagine that some mammals are large animals, then I cannot avoid imagining that these same large animals are mammals, and consequently, that the statement "Some large animals are mammals" is true. This is no great surprise to me — I already knew this. So, in this case, the sound argument did not give me any new knowledge. But sometimes sound reasoning reveals great and important truths that *we* did not know previously, or even sometimes, truths that *no one* knew previously. Sound reasoning may also sometimes be used to explain events that we knew occurred, but did not know why.

SUMMARY OF DEFINITIONS OF BASIC TERMS

Valid reasoning: Reasoning in which the reasons, if they were true, really would justify believing or expecting the conclusion to be true. In valid reasoning, the truth of the statement(s) given as the reason(s) (supposing they were true) would guarantee, or make extremely likely, the truth of the conclusion.

Invalid reasoning: Reasoning in which the reasons, even assuming or supposing they were true, still would not justify believing or expecting the conclusion to be true.

Sound reasoning: Reasoning in which the steps of reasoning are valid and all relevant reasons are true.

Unsound reasoning: Reasoning in which either one (or more) of the relevant reasons is false, or the step of inference is invalid, or both.

Degrees of Validity (or Degrees of Confirmation)

A given step of inference may be valid or invalid, depending on how likely the truth of the reasons (if they were true) would make the truth of the conclusion. Within the scope of these two possibilities, it is useful to distinguish *five* different extents to which the truth of the reason(s) may confirm (or fail to confirm) the truth of a conclusion. These can be called "degrees of confirmation," "degrees of support," or "degrees of validity" (as I call them). Being able to work with them accurately in real world applications is more important than the terminology. These five degrees are: *nil, weak, moderate, strong,* and *deductively valid.* These are approximate categories that roughly correspond to various ranges along a scale of values going from 0% to 100% confirmation, like this:

DEGREES OF VALIDITY

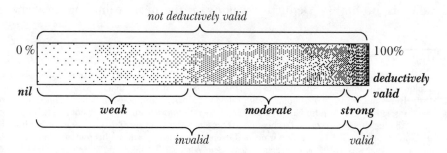

The degree of validity (or "degree of confirmation") of an inference can be estimated as follows: Suppose, pretend, or imagine, that the statements immediately above the arrow in the given diagram all were true, and then ask yourself, "How likely, in that case, would it be that the statement shown as the conclusion below the arrow is true?" Starting with the highest, the five different degrees of validity (or "support," "confirmation," or whatever you want to call them) are as follows:

1. **Deductively valid:** If the truth of the reason(s) would *totally guarantee* the truth of the conclusion, the inference rates as "deductively valid" (and so, of

course, as "valid"). In order for an inference to be "deductively valid," it must be absolutely *impossible* for anyone to think of *any* conceivable way — no matter how far-fetched — in which the reason(s) could be true and yet the conclusion be false. Here is an extremely simple example:

This piece of glass is blue.

↓ *(deductively valid)*

This piece of glass is colored.

The rating "deductively valid" is written *alongside the arrow* where "valid" was written before, because the evaluation "deductively valid" is a slightly more precise evaluation than just "valid." This step of inference is rated as deductively valid *as it stands,* because if the given premise is true, then the conclusion cannot fail to be true too.[1] If one assumes or supposes that the premise "This piece of glass is blue" is true, then it is impossible to think of any imaginable way in which the conclusion could at the same time be false. [2]

   If someone claims that a step of reasoning is deductively valid but some-one else can describe a conceivable way in which the given conclusion could be false while the given reason(s) were true, that possibility, even though it may exist only in the imagination, is enough to show that the rating "deductively valid" is too high. "Deductive validity" is the perfect limiting case where the

---

[1] *Note to Advanced Readers:* Although it is not formally deductively valid, this inference is as certain as any formally valid argument, because in English, the statement "This glass is blue" semantically entails "This glass is colored." Some intransigent advocates of formal approaches may insist that in declaring this inference to be deductively valid, we are at least implicitly appealing to hidden assumptions, and that it cannot be regarded as valid in isolation. But as John Nolt well puts it, "there is no more justification for holding that the necessary truth 'All blue things are colored' is needed to complete [this inference] than there is for holding that the necessary truth $((A \supset B)$ & $A) \supset B$ is needed to complete instances of modus ponens. And Lewis Carroll showed us what was wrong with the latter idea. (See 'What the Tortoise Said to Achilles,' *Mind* 4, 1895, pp. 278-280.)" See Nolt, "Possible Worlds and Imagination in Informal Logic," *Informal Logic,* vi, 2 (July 1984), p. 17.

[2] *Note to Advanced Readers:* The explication of "deductively valid" inferences as those in which the conclusion is true in every logically possible world in which the premises are true is obviously also the basic conception underlying the formal definition of deductively valid argument schemata as those in which the conclusion comes out true on every interpretation of the schematic letters on which the premises come out true. This conception was generalized in the first (1973) and subsequent editions of *Practical Reasoning in Natural Language* so that it would apply universally and directly to all reasoning in natural languages. One refinement was to handle degrees of confirmation by considering, in effect, the probability as well as number of possible worlds in which the reason(s) came out true but the conclusion is false. To ask "Is there any possible way in which the premise(s) could be true and yet the conclusion be false, and if so, how likely are they?" is a simpler and more ontologically parsimonious way of expressing the same question, a form of speech more appealing to nominalists.

connection between the reason(s) and the conclusion is so iron-clad that there is no conceivable way, no matter how unlikely, in which the reason(s) could be true and yet the conclusion be false — not even if there occurred a sudden reversal of the law of gravity, or an invasion by extra-terrestrials in spaceships, or any other highly unlikely circumstance.

Since, as explained earlier, the validity requirement is not the same as the requirement that the reasons be true, even reasoning with false premises can be deductively valid. This happens when the conclusion is related to the false reason(s) in such a way that the reason(s) could not be true without the conclusion being true too. The silly example about dogs flying with their ears, for instance, is deductively valid:

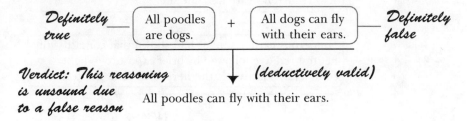

If you imagine it true that "All dogs can fly with their ears" and that "All poodles are dogs," there is no way in which you can avoid also imagining it true that "All poodles can fly with their ears." The falseness of one of the reasons does not prevent the reasoning from being deductively valid (but it does prevent it from being sound and so it prevents the argument from proving this silly conclusion).

2. **Strong:** In real life, it would be impractical and unrealistic to require or expect every inference to be deductively valid before accepting its conclusion as proven or explained. Usually we need only for the degree of validity to be high enough for all practical human purposes. If the truth of some reason(s) would make the truth of a drawn conclusion overwhelmingly likely — that is, establishing it beyond any reasonable doubt and making its truth so likely that we can rely on it for all practical purposes — then the step of inference is rated as "strong" and it is considered valid. (Traditional logicians sometimes call such inferences "inductively valid.") When an inference is rated as "strong," this means that there may be some conceivable ways in which the reason(s) could be true and yet the conclusion be false, *but they are extremely unlikely*, and not the kind of thing that occurs in the real world (or at least, not very often).

For instance, after a series of clinical trials to test the effectiveness of one of the early treatments for *herpes simplex* involving painting the sores with neutral red dye (NA 676) and then irradiating them with ordinary light, medical researchers reasoned as follows.[1] (In this example, because of the length of the sentences, the reasons have been written in a vertical rather than horizontal list; this makes absolutely no difference to the reasoning.)

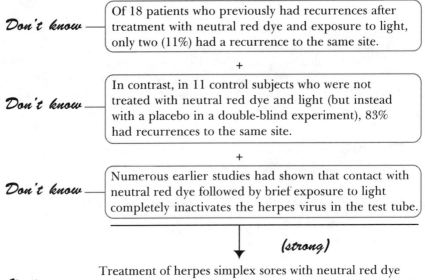

Don't know — Of 18 patients who previously had recurrences after treatment with neutral red dye and exposure to light, only two (11%) had a recurrence to the same site.

+

Don't know — In contrast, in 11 control subjects who were not treated with neutral red dye and light (but instead with a placebo in a double-blind experiment), 83% had recurrences to the same site.

+

Don't know — Numerous earlier studies had shown that contact with neutral red dye followed by brief exposure to light completely inactivates the herpes virus in the test tube.

(strong)

Verdict:
Can't say   Treatment of herpes simplex sores with neutral red dye and light alters or eliminates the virus at the site treated, rendering it less likely to produce a new sore at exactly the same site.

Here the cited reasons give "strong" support to the conclusion. They do not, of course, establish it conclusively, or with total or absolute certainty — the evidence *could* imaginably be as described and yet this treatment be ineffective against the virus (the observed results might be due entirely to chance, or to the action of some other hidden cause). However, this seems unlikely. Certainly the evidence supports the conclusion strongly enough to justify acting as if that conclusion were true (assuming, of course, that the reasons given are true).

In this example, I found it easier to decide how to rate the degree of validity of the inference than to decide about the truth or falsity of the reasons. With regard to the truth or falsity of the reasons, I found myself wavering between saying "Probably true" and saying "Uncertain/Don't know." At first, I was strongly tempted to say "Probably true" because I found myself inclined to trust these three statements to be an accurate report of the experimenters' observations, but finally I decided that I actually should say "Don't know" because I had heard about these reports indirectly from only one source, and it

---

[1] Troy D. Felber and others, "Photodynamic Inactivation of Herpes Simplex, Report of a Clinical Trial," *Journal of the American Medical Association*, 223, no. 3, 292.

seems to be a genuine possibility that I may not have gotten the facts quite right, or that there may have been other sources of inaccuracy. Of course, *if* I made the effort to dig deeper, and do more investigating, I *might* become able to reclassify these statements confidently as "Probably true." (Perhaps you know more about this topic than I do, so that you may be able to put them into another category.) Since I do not know whether these reasons are true or false, I cannot say whether this reasoning is sound or unsound, as I indicated in my "verdict." The reasoning meets the validity requirement, but whether it meets the requirement of having all true reasons, I honestly do not know. Before accepting a conclusion as proven, one must be able to rate all the reasons as at least "Probably true," and rate the step of reasoning as either "deductively valid" or "strong". [1]

3. **Moderate:** In other cases, the reasons, if true, would provide only "moderate" support for the drawn conclusion. For example, the following reasoning was widely heard back in the 1970's:

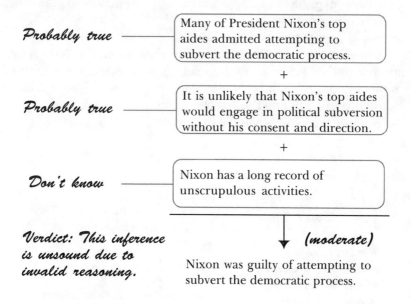

The reasons given in this example provide significant support for the conclusion,

---

[1]*Note to Advanced Readers:* In the present approach, the term "valid" is used to describe both deductively valid and strong inferences, a way of speaking that departs from some traditional terminologies in which the term "valid" was reserved for deductively valid inferences and not applied to strong inferences that are less than deductively valid. The traditional terminology arose, in part, from extensionalism and the questionable presupposition of a fundamental induction-deduction dichotomy.

but they do not prove it conclusively, or beyond any reasonable doubt. [1] Although perhaps unlikely, it is still possible (as far as the reasons given here are concerned) that Nixon's top aides acted as they did without his consent and direction, so that, despite his past behavior, he is innocent of the charge. The truth of the reasons would make the truth of the conclusion "a good bet," but they fall short of establishing it beyond a reasonable doubt, or as a "sure thing." (Notice that the test of validity given earlier — if reasoning is valid, it should not be possible to imagine any realistic way in which the reasons could be true and yet the conclusion be false — again is being applied here to make this judgment.) So although this reasoning has moderate strength, *more* evidence (the "White-House tapes," for example?) would be needed to make it valid and establish guilt beyond any reasonable doubt.

"So, should we accept such reasoning or not?" In answer to this question, I would say that the cited evidence certainly gives enough support to the conclusion to justify *suspecting* Nixon's guilt and requesting a further investigation, but that these reasons alone, *by themselves,* give insufficient support to the conclusion to justify accepting it as true or proven. Proving the conclusion requires more evidence than this.

It should be remembered that the rating *"moderate"* here relates only to the degree of validity (or confirmation) of this reasoning. It is NOT a rating of the truth, nor of the likelihood, of the reason(s) or conclusion being true. It is only a rating of how much the premises, *if they be true,* would make it likely that the conclusion is true. In other words, it is a rating of the goodness of the *logical connection* between the reasons and the conclusion.

4. **Weak:** In some arguments, the reasons provide only weak support for the conclusion. Here is an example:

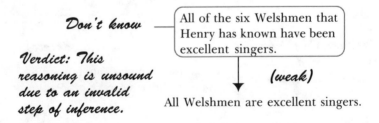

Don't know — All of the six Welshmen that Henry has known have been excellent singers.

Verdict: This reasoning is unsound due to an invalid step of inference.

(weak)

All Welshmen are excellent singers.

---

[1] It should be remembered, as explained earlier, that various evaluators with different background knowledge can properly give different appraisals of the likely truth or falsity of the same statement. The ratings in the illustrations only show what I believe I know about these statements. I may have rated some of them incorrectly, and someone else might be able to prove this with another argument. But if I have gotten some of them wrong, this in itself shows no defect in the methods, but only errors in what I thought I knew about Nixon, herpes, etc. No sound logical methodology purports to confer infallibility on its practitioners, and it would be absurd to expect otherwise.

This inference is weak because it draws a conclusion about a very large group of individuals (*all* people from the country of Wales) based on information about only six members of that group. It is too hasty a generalization. Furthermore, no indication is given that these six individuals were randomly chosen or that they are representative of the group of Welshmen as a whole. Notice that classifying this step of reasoning as "weak" does *not* mean that Welshmen are not all excellent singers. It still might be true that all Welshmen are excellent singers, but the evidence cited here as a reason fails to prove it. This is all that is meant when we say that the degree of validity is weak. Notice, too, that it's NOT because I happen to be ignorant as to whether the premise is true or false (since I do not know Henry) that the inference is weak. It would be equally weak even if I happened to know for certain that the premise were true. It is weak because the evidence given in the reason falls far short of proving the truth of the generalization in the conclusion. Its weakness is shown by the *real possibility of the conclusion's being false even if the reason given is true.* Although this step of reasoning is *weak*, it is not a total zero, because the reason does give a tiny bit of evidence of the sort that is relevant to proving the truth of such a conclusion.

It would be a confusion to oppose this reason for the validity evaluation with the following argument:

> *Objection:* "You say that the reasoning in this Welshman argument is weak because it is possible for the conclusion to be false. However, it is also possible for the conclusion to be true. It is possible that all Welshmen are excellent singers. So, isn't the situation really more of an equal standoff? The conclusion might be true, or it might be false. Shouldn't you, then, give a neutral evaluation, or say that you "can't tell," rather than giving a negative evaluation like 'weak'?"

This objection involves several fundamental misunderstandings. First of all, anyone who correctly evaluates the degree of confirmation or validity of an inference is doing something far deeper and more complex than merely trying to judge the likelihood that the conclusion is false. If the objector will look again at the preceding discussion, it will be seen that I never said that "the Welshman argument is weak because it is possible for the conclusion to be false." That may be what the objector thought I said, but this misquotes and misunderstands what was said. Instead, the Welshman argument is evaluated as "weak" because it is easily possible *for the reason to be true AND for the conclusion to be false AT THE SAME TIME,* something different, deeper, and more complicated than simply saying that it is possible for the conclusion to be false.

Evaluating the validity of an inference is different from simply judging the likelihood of the conclusion's being true. In judging the degree of confirmation (or "degree of validity") of an inference, we are NOT simply appraising the likelihood that the conclusion is true. When we evaluate an inference as "weak," for example, we are *not* saying that the conclusion is uncertain or probably false, and when we evaluate an inference as "strong," we are *not* saying that the conclusion is probably true. Rather, we are evaluating the *reliability* of the *step of inference* from the reason(s) to the conclusion. We are judging the strength, or goodness, of the *connection between* the reason(s) and the conclusion. We are not evaluating the *statements* below and above the arrow, but rather the strength of the *arrow* itself between them.

When logicians call reasoning "invalid," they are not saying that the conclusion is false or uncertain. They are saying that the conclusion does not follow logically from the reason(s). Talk of "validity" and "invalidity" concerns whether the step of reasoning represented by the arrow is solid and reliable. And this is NOT determined by asking how likely is the truth of the conclusion, BUT RATHER, by asking how likely the truth of the reasons, if true, WOULD MAKE the truth of the conclusion. This is judged NOT by asking "Is it possible for the conclusion to be false?," but rather by asking, "Is it possible for the reason(s) to be true and yet the conclusion be false?" The question we ask in judging validity or invalidity is NOT whether there is any realistic way in which the conclusion could be false. Instead, in judging validity, we ask whether we can think of any realistic way(s) in which it could happen *both* that all the reasons be true *and*, at the same time, the conclusion be false. For example, in the Welshman argument, the step of inference is weak NOT because the conclusion ("All Welshmen are excellent singers") can easily be imagined false; RATHER, the inference is weak because we can easily imagine this conclusion being false while the reason ("All of the six Welshmen that Henry has known have been excellent singers") is true. The weakness of the inference is shown by the fact that it is *quite possible for the conclusion to be false even if the reason is true.* To be valid, the reason (or reasons) need to be related to the conclusion in such a way that, if true, their truth would effectively eliminate any real possibility of the conclusion's being false.

The following new objection may now arise, stemming from a different confusion:

> Objection: "You say that the reasoning in the Welshman example is weak because it is possible for the conclusion to be *false* even if the reason(s) be true. But in this example, it is also possible for the conclusion to be *true* if the reasons be true. If it is true that "All six Welshmen that Henry has known have been excellent singers," it is possible for the conclusion ("All Welshmen are excellent singers") still to be true. So, isn't the situation still really a standoff? If the reason is true, the conclusion might be true or it might be false. So, shouldn't

the argument be given a neutral evaluation — Shouldn't we say that
we 'can't tell,' rather than giving a negative evaluation like 'weak'?"
Here another fundamental misunderstanding needs correction. In order for reasoning to be "valid," any real possibility of the conclusion's being false *needs to be eliminated by the reason(s)*. This is the *job* of the reason(s) in sound reasoning. Logic is concerned with eliminating — or at least minimizing — any real danger of mistakenly arriving at false conclusions This is why the question whether or not the truth of the reasons would practically guarantee the truth of the conclusion is so important.

The existence of any real possibility of an argument's conclusion being false even though the reasons be true shows that the truth of the reasons would not eliminate the possibility of the conclusion's being false. This is why the mere existence of such a possibility makes the inference invalid and shows that the truth of the conclusion has not yet been proven. When such a possibility exists, the argument has failed to guarantee the truth of its conclusion and is invalid, because the truth of the reasons, if they be true, would not eliminate all genuine danger or risk of the conclusion's being false.[1]

5. **Nil:** At the lowest end of the spectrum comes reasoning in which the reasons provide *no* support whatsoever for the drawn conclusion. Here is an example:

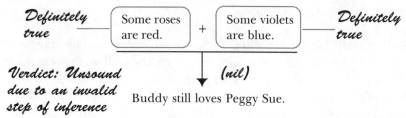

The reasons in this argument provide not even the slightest support for the drawn conclusion. In such a case, the degree of validity (or "degree of confirmation") is rated as "*nil.*"

Notice that this rating, like all the other ratings of degrees of confirmation, is *WRITTEN BESIDE THE ARROW!* This is done because the arrow represents the step of reasoning, or inference, between the reason(s) and conclusion, of which this is the evaluation. When students write validity ratings elsewhere than beside the arrow, it often indicates that they do not really

---

[1]Of course, if someone were trying to prove that the statement in the position of the conclusion is *false,* rather than proving it true, *then* in that case, we would focus on the question mentioned in the objection (that is, whether it is possible for "All Welshmen are excellent singers" to be true if the reasons given are true).

understand what they are doing. The term "nil" describes the extent to which the reasons *if true* would render the conclusion probable, and *NOT* the probable truth or falsity of the reason(s) or conclusion. The probable truth or falsity of the reasons is rated separately with the circles ("lassos") and terms like "Definitely true," "Probably true," etc.. Of course, both considerations enter into our judgment regarding the argument's soundness or unsoundness.

In summary, to evaluate the *degree of validity (or degree of confirmation)* of any inference, ask **the magic question:** Is there any imaginable way in which the conclusion could be false even if (or even though) the reason(s) be true? And if so, how likely is it? An alternative way to express the same question is to ask whether it is possible to conceive of a world in which the premises would be true, and yet the conclusion be false. If the answer to this question is "No," then the inference rates as "deductively valid." If the answer to this question is "Yes," one next asks the question: How likely is the most likely of these possibilities? If every such possible way is *highly unlikely*, then the degree of confirmation rates as "strong," and the inference still rates as "valid." But if one or more of these imaginable ways is a genuine possibility — a situation of the sort that has a real possibility or likelihood of arising in the real world — then the inference rates as "invalid," and the degree of validity is "moderate" or "weak," depending on the likelihood of these conceivable circumstances, or "nil" if the reasons give no support whatsoever to the conclusion.[1]

6. **Can't tell:** Finally, the category "can't tell" is reserved for those *extremely rare* cases in which we cannot determine how likely the truth of the reasons would make the truth of the conclusion. This rating is not intended to be used simply because some person is too lazy to think carefully and accurately about the degree of validity of a given inference. If students write that they "can't tell" the degree of validity when actually it is within their ability to determine it, then

---

[1]In the methods introduced in *PRNL* (1973) we not only ask the number of possible worlds in which the premises are true but also the conclusion false, and *consider their probability.* Endless concrete counter-examples show the fallaciousness of John Nolt's proposed alternative method of attempting to determine degrees of validity by considering the totality of possible worlds in which the premise(s) are true, and then rating the degree of validity as "strong" if the statement expressing the conclusion is true in a high proportion of these possible worlds, and weak if it is false in most of them. For instance, the *"nil-to-weak"* inference "The Earth has at least one moon; therefore, the Earth has more than a billion moons" inaccurately receives the rating *"strong"* by Nolt's proposed criterion, while strong statistical generalizations from adequate samplings and other strong inductive inferences get misevaluated as *"weak to nil."* The fallaciousness of Nolt's method is shown in "Degrees of Validity and Ratios of Conceivable Worlds," *Informal Logic,* 6, 3 (December 1984), 31-34, and by Howard Kahane in "John Nolt's Inductive Reasoning Test, *ibid.*, 30-31. This is probably of little import to instructors who care not whether the methods of logic they teach are sound (or who cannot discern the difference), but I believe that *unsound* methods should *not* be taught in logic courses despite being easy, convenient, and fashionable.

"can't tell" is a mistaken answer, because they could tell. Inferences should be placed in the "can't tell" category only in those highly unusual cases in which one really cannot determine whether or not it is possible for the conclusion to be false if the reasons are true.

Most examples of "can't tell" inferences are found in abstruse theoretical subjects like mathematics and philosophy. In mathematics, for example, there are some claims that *appear to be* universally true, but which have never been proven. For example, in the theory of whole numbers, there are unproven mathematical claims or theorems that hold true for all the numbers on which they have been tested with computers, but since they are only a limited finite subset from the infinity of numbers, this is inconclusive with regard to the question whether they hold in every case. One famous simple example is "Goldbach's Conjecture," which says that every even whole number is the sum of two prime numbers.[1] If someone exhibited an argument diagram in which the premises were the axioms of elementary number theory, and the conclusion was Goldbach's Conjecture, and asked me (or anyone I know) to evaluate the degree of validity of a step of inference from these axioms to this conclusion, we would have to say that we "can't tell." The given conclusion might follow logically, or it might not, for all that we can tell. A gifted mathematician may someday successfully fill in intermediate conclusions between these axioms and this final conclusion in a series of steps each of which is obviously deductively valid, thereby proving Goldbach's Conjecture — or someone may find a number that is a counter-example to the universal Goldbach Conjecture, thereby proving that the it is not true. Until that day, however, the rest of us must confess ourselves unable to tell whether Goldbach's Conjecture follows logically from the axioms of arithmetic. However, none of the exercises at the end of this section falls into the "can't tell" category, so do not worry about it now.

Summary of Degrees of Validity
(or "Degrees of Confirmation")

Deductively valid: There is no conceivable or imaginable way in which the reason(s) could be true and yet the conclusion be false. Truth of the premise(s) would totally guarantee the truth of the conclusion. It is logically impossible for the reason(s) to be true and the conclusion false.

Strong: If the reasons were true, they would make the truth of the conclusion extremely likely, certain beyond any reasonable doubt, "virtually a sure

---

[1] Goldbach conjectured (but could not prove) that every even whole number is the sum of two prime numbers. (A "prime number" is any whole number that is evenly divisible, without remainder, only by itself and the number 1.) So, for example, as Goldbach conjectured, the even number 2 is the sum of the two prime numbers 1 and 1, $4 = 3 + 1$, $6 = 5 + 1$, $8 = 5 + 3$, and so on.

thing," but not totally guaranteed. (How likely is "extremely likely"? Likely enough to make it reasonable to stake something of great value on the truth of the conclusion if the reasons are true, and likely enough to serve as a definitely reliable basis for actions.)

Moderate: Less than "strong" but more than "weak." If the reasons were true, they would not establish the truth of the conclusion as "a sure thing," but they would at least make it "a good bet." However, *more* would be required to establish the conclusion beyond any reasonable doubt.

Weak: If the given reasons were true, then they would provide a small amount of support for the conclusion, but not enough to justify accepting the conclusion as true. The reasons are logically relevant to the conclusion, making it a "live possibility," but they are not strong enough even to make it "a good bet."

Nil: Even if all the given reasons were true, they would provide no justification whatsoever for the conclusion.

NOTE: There is room for individual judgments to vary in applying these ratings. They are approximate. The absence of sharp boundaries between these different degrees actually enhances their utility in application to reasoning in natural language, the data, for no sharp boundary exists there either.

3. Clarifying Language when Evaluating Reasoning

Before evaluating the soundness of reasoning, sometimes it is necessary to clarify the meaning of some of the language involved, because if we do not know what some statements in the diagram mean, we cannot determine whether the reasoning is sound or unsound, since we do not know exactly what is being said.

Consider, for example, the following reasoning:

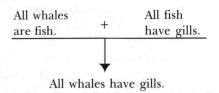

When trying to evaluate this argument, a question arises whether the word "fish" is being used in the *precise zoological* sense of "a cold-blooded, strictly aquatic, water-breathing vertebrate animal having the limbs developed as fins," or is "fish" being used in the *broad, loose sense* of "almost any exclusively aquatic animal with fins," or what? When we are presented with such a choice of interpretations, the *"Principle of Charity"* says: If possible, choose the interpretation, or meaning of the words, that makes the reasoning come out sound. In this example, however, this cannot be done because if I interpret "fish" in the precise zoological sense, the first reason comes out false while the second reason comes out true — and, if I interpret "fish" in the loose broad sense, the first reason comes out true, but the second reason comes out false (because whales are warm-blooded and have lungs). Finally, if "fish" were interpreted in the *loose, broad sense* in the *left-hand reason*, while taking it in the *precise zoological sense* in the *right-hand reason,* then although each reason would come out true, the *step of inference* would be invalid, due to a "fallacy of equivocation."[1] So, there is no way to interpret the language in the argument so as to make the reasoning come out sound. In other examples, however, as will be seen later, reasoning can be unsound on one interpretation, but sound on another interpretation. In such a case, the Principle of Charity says to choose the interpretation on which the reasoning comes out sound.

When the meaning of unclear language in a diagram needs to be clarified, this may be done by adding a footnote that specifies the meaning that the unclear terminology is understood to have for the purpose of evaluating the reasoning. For example, if I am going to evaluate the reasoning about whales with the unclear term "fish" understood in the broad sense, this can be shown with a footnote as follows:

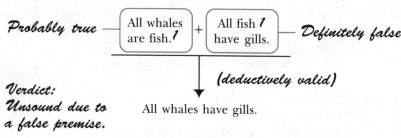

Probably true — All whales are fish.[1] + All fish[1] have gills. — *Definitely false*

(deductively valid)

Verdict:
Unsound due to
a false premise.

All whales have gills.

1. I am taking "fish" in the broad sense of
"almost any exclusively aquadic animal with fins."

If I had used a footnote to show that I was interpreting the word "fish" in its precise zoological interpretation, the reasoning would still be unsound (because the left-hand reason would now be false). And if I had chosen to interpret "fish" in a loose sense in the left-hand reason and in its precise zoological sense in the

---

[1]The term "fallacy" is used in logic to describe reasoning that is defective or deficient in some way. The *fallacy of equivocation* occurs when, in the course of reasoning, the *meanings of crucial words change* in such a way as to make the conclusion *appear* to follow logically, when actually it does *not* follow. This will be explained in more detail later.

right-hand reason, this could be shown with two footnotes, numbered "1" and "2." If preferred, instead of footnotes, one can replace any unclear language with clearer language shown in square brackets.

Collateral Information

In reasoning, some assumed reasons or background assumptions often are left unstated and taken to be "understood." When appropriate, they may be added to the diagram [enclosing them in square brackets, like this, to show that they are something that has been added]. In general, it is appropriate to add further reasons to a diagram and evaluate the reasoning with them included whenever (i) it is reasonable to believe that the author or original proponent of the reasoning intends, or would intend, to be making these additional assumptions, or (ii) you yourself know that these additional statements are true and adding them to the diagram increases the strength of the inference. But it is often impractical to try to write in every background assumption presupposed in typical reasoning, because there are too many and it would take too long.[1] So, in real cases, we sometimes operate as if certain "understood" additional statements were written in along with the given reasons. In such cases, you are permitted simply to include them mentally, in your mind. But if any question, dispute, or problem may arise regarding any of these additional assumptions, then any controversial ones need to be written in clearly so that they can be considered explicitly.

4. Soundness and Reliability Verdicts

If all relevant reasons are "definitely true" and the step of inference from them to a conclusion is valid, then the reasoning is sound and reliable. But if one or more of the reasons is false, *or* if the step of reasoning is invalid, then the reasoning fails to prove or explain the conclusion and it is unsound and unreliable. (It should always be remembered, of course that the conclusion of unsound, unreliable reasoning still can happen to be true; calling reasoning "unsound" only means that it fails to prove or explain the truth of its conclusion; it does not necessarily mean that the conclusion is false.)

What about all other possible situations? The following table shows how they are evaluated. The abbreviations used in the table have the following meanings:

---

[1] Some contemporary logicians and philosophers of science have suggested that many inferences in natural language, including scientific inferences, ultimately presuppose, as background assumptions, most of the totality of the rest of our knowledge and beliefs, a totality so large that actually writing down all these assumptions would be a hopeless project.

S	=	The reasoning is sound and reliable.
P S	=	The reasoning is probably sound and reliable.
M	=	The reasoning is marginal; it is close to being sound and reliable, but not quite certain or totally reliable beyond a reasonable doubt.
C S	=	We cannot say whether the reasoning is sound or unsound (and so, we should not rely on it).
P U	=	The reasoning is probably unsound and unreliable.
U	=	The reasoning is unsound and unreliable.

To use the table, give the verdict that appears in the box where the horizontal row corresponding to the rating of the truth of the reason(s) intersects with the vertical column corresponding to the degree of confirmation or validity rating:

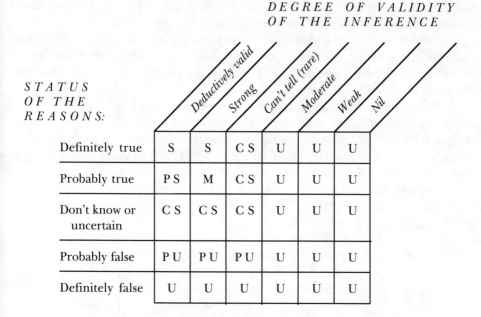

DEGREE OF VALIDITY OF THE INFERENCE

STATUS OF THE REASONS:	Deductively valid	Strong	Can't tell (rare)	Moderate	Weak	Nil
Definitely true	S	S	C S	U	U	U
Probably true	P S	M	C S	U	U	U
Don't know or uncertain	C S	C S	C S	U	U	U
Probably false	P U	P U	P U	U	U	U
Definitely false	U	U	U	U	U	U

TABLE OF SOUNDNESS AND RELIABILITY VERDICTS

NOTES: When the reason(s) rate only "Probably true" but the inference is *deductively valid,* we cannot say for certain that the reasoning is sound, because unknown to us, the "probably true" reason(s) might actually be false, and hence the reasoning might actually be unsound; however, this is unlikely, and hence the reasoning rates as "Probably sound and reliable (P S)."

When the reason(s) rate only "Probably true" and the inference is strong, the uncertainty about the truth of the reason(s) is compounded by the possibility of error arising from an inference that is less than totally certain. The reliability of the reasoning is lowered to the gray or borderline area between being reliable and not being reliable, so the verdict is that the reasoning is "Marginal." The mutual presence of *both* these two small dangers of error together increases the risk of drawing an erroneous conclusion enough to bring the reliability of the reasoning down to the gray area between being reliable and not being reliable.

When the reason(s) are rated as "Probably false" but the inference is deductively valid, there is a tiny chance that the "Probably false" reason(s) will turn out to be true. (For example, it is "probably false" that the next cut of the cards will be the Ace of Hearts, but it could happen.) So since it is unlikely that a probably false reason will turn out to be true, the verdict is "Probably unsound and unreliable." Remember that this does not mean that the conclusion is false, but only that we cannot count on its being true.

If the inference is valid but we "Don't know" or are "Uncertain" about the truth of the reason(s), or if we are confident that the reasons are true, but "Can't tell" whether the inference is valid or invalid, then we "Can't say" whether the reasoning is sound or unsound.

Situations in which we "Can't tell" whether the inference is valid or invalid are rare, but situations in which we "Don't know" or are "Uncertain" about the truth or falsity of the reason(s) are the most common of all. If one doesn't know, or can't tell about either, then naturally one "can't say" whether the reasoning sound or unsound. In such a case, of course, one cannot rely on it either.

In philosophy, major efforts sometimes are made to transform reasoning that rates as "Marginal" or "Can't say" into reasoning that is either clearly sound or clearly unsound.

Examples

Example 1: George has several suitcases, so therefore George has some luggage.   — Adapted from G. E. Moore

Don't know ——— George has several suitcases.

                                    ↓ *(deductively valid)*

Verdict:
Can't   George has some luggage.

This reasoning is deductively valid as it stands, because the meanings of "luggage" and "suitcase" in English guarantee that if it is true that a person has several suitcases, then the conclusion is unavoidable that this person also has some luggage. For, by the meanings of these terms, "suitcases" are instances of "luggage." So the reasoning is deductively valid as it stands. However, I must write "Don't know" beside the given premise, because I do not know the person to whom the name 'George' here refers, nor do I know whether this person has any suitcases. So consequently, I "Can't say" whether the reasoning is sound or unsound.

Example 2: According to a recent article in the highly respected scientific journal, *Physical Review,* magnets having only one pole ("magnetic monopoles") exist. Therefore, magnets having only one pole exist.

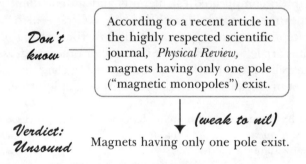

Don't know — According to a recent article in the highly respected scientific journal, *Physical Review,* magnets having only one pole ("magnetic monopoles") exist.

Verdict:
Unsound   ↓ *(weak to nil)*
                    Magnets having only one pole exist.

It was easy to write "Don't know" beside the reason, because I do not know whether such an article was published in that journal or not. If I had seen and read it, then I would know whether such an article appeared, but since I did not, I must say that I do not know whether a journal by that name carried such an article.

The step of inference rates as "weak to nil," because the mere fact that such an article had been published (which is all that the reason says) would not prove that magnetic monopoles exist. The proof of a claim about the existence of magnetic monopoles must be based on the observations and theories of science, rather than based on the fact that such an article has appeared. It would be absurd to think that a claim in physics could be proven simply by being published (even in a prestigious journal), or that someone could correctly or justifiably claim to *know* it to be definitely true, or even probably true, simply because he or she had read it in such a publication. Competent researchers in physics would consider it ridiculous to think that publication of a claim in physics constitutes evidence, or an acceptable substitute for experimental evidence, that the claim is true. (If the mere fact of its publication constituted adequate evidence of the truth of a claim in science, there would be no need for scientists to labor in laboratories to prove or disprove scientific claims; they would need only ink, paper, and a printing press to confirm scientific theories by publishing them.)

Similarly, it would be foolish for anyone to say that he or she knows, for example, a claim of physics, to be "probably true" on mere grounds of publication that experts with more knowledge of physics would regard as completely insufficient. To maintain that one knows this claim to be true on such a basis when competent physicists would say that they still do not know whether the claim is true would be silly. Scientific claims can only be proven by an appeal to theoretical and experimental considerations, and not by an appeal to authority — not even the authority of a respected scientific magazine. The editors and reviewers for even the most prestigious journals do not, in general, have the time or resources to do complicated calculations and independent replications of elaborate experiments to double-check the accuracy of articles prior to publication. Replications of experiments and further testing of theories and published claims are left open as future projects for other readers of the journal and other researchers in the field. So, the fact that a claim has been published in even the most prestigious journal does not prove that it is true.

Example 3: Processed meats contain less sodium than processed cheese. So processed meats are a food that is relatively low in sodium, as compared with other foods.
— Adapted from an advertisement in the *New England Journal of Medicine.*

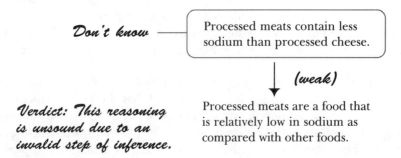

Don't know ——— Processed meats contain less sodium than processed cheese.

↓ *(weak)*

Verdict: This reasoning is unsound due to an invalid step of inference.

Processed meats are a food that is relatively low in sodium as compared with other foods.

The reason given provides only "weak" support for the conclusion drawn, because it is easy for the reason to be true and the conclusion to be false. This could happen, for example, if processed cheese, the only food cited as the basis for comparison, actually had a very high sodium content. If so, then processed meats could contain less sodium than processed cheese, and yet still be relatively high in sodium content. So the inference is invalid. However, there is a tiny bit of information, or evidence, here of the right general kind to support this conclusion, so the degree of confirmation (degree of validity) is not quite "nil." Thus the inference rates as "weak." Although I do not know whether the statement given as the reason is true or false, I know that the invalidity of the reasoning makes it unsound, which is my verdict.

I wrote "Don't know" beside the circle around the statement "Processed meats contain less sodium than processed cheese" because I do not know whether it is true or false. To argue that I know it to be true because it appeared in an advertisement in the prestigious *New England Journal of Medicine* would be unsound reasoning. Such reasoning would commit the fallacy of "appeal to authority," which is the logical error of inappropriately concluding that some statement is true because some supposed expert, authority, or publication said that it is true. The fallacy of "appeal to authority" occurs when someone inappropriately uses the fact that some alleged authority, expert, famous person, or publication agrees with a claim as a justification for thinking that it is true. Even when the cited "authority" is known to be a genuine expert on the topic, speaking sincerely with no bias or personal vested interest in the matter, if the question is whether the opinion of this expert is correct, the fact that the expert holds this opinion does not settle the question of correctness. Even the great physicist Einstein would have agreed that the fact that he holds a certain opinion on a question in physics is no proof that the opinion is correct. Great thinkers and experts can be sincerely mistaken, and the proof or disproof of their views is to be found in whatever independent, objective reasons or evidence confirm or disconfirm to these views.

Example 4: Laetrile contains cyanide, and cyanide is a deadly poison. Therefore, laetrile could not be effective as a cure for cancer.

—Adapted from a United States Postal Office government publication.

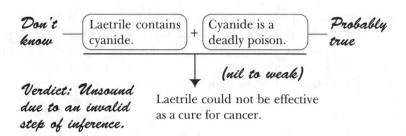

These reasons, as they stand, provide almost no support for this conclusion, because it is quite easy for them to be true, and yet the conclusion be false. This could happen, for example, if any cyanide in laetrile were contained in a form that permitted only cancerous cells to be poisoned by it. (Effective medicines sometimes are selective poisons — selective against diseased cells or undesired micro-organisms.) The reasoning is so weak as to be almost nil, so I rated it somewhere in-between.

Remember that when reasoning is rated as unsound, this does *not* mean that we are saying that the conclusion is false! To classify reasoning as "unsound" only means that *the conclusion is not justified or explained by the reasons given*. Judging a piece of reasoning to be unsound *leaves it open* whether the conclusion is true or false. The conclusion of unsound reasoning might still be true, and some *other reasoning* might even prove it. When we say that reasoning is unsound, we are only saying that the given reasons do not, by themselves, prove or explain the truth of the conclusion. We are not thereby saying that the conclusion is false.

> **Example 5:** Since I am convinced that an artist can have no greater
> enemies than his bad paintings, I do not release a painting or drawing
> until I have given it every possible effort.
>
>> — From a radio interview with Henri Matisse, first broadcast in 1942,
>> translated by Pierre Schneider, quoted from Jack D. Flam, *Matisse on Art*
>> (Oxford: Phaidon Press, 1973; New York: E.P. Dutton, 1973), p. 92.

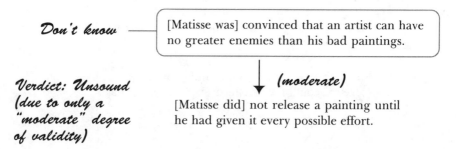

Don't know ——— [Matisse was] convinced that an artist can have no greater enemies than his bad paintings.

(moderate)

Verdict: Unsound (due to only a "moderate" degree of validity)

[Matisse did] not release a painting until he had given it every possible effort.

Here, in this explanation which is also a justification, the step of inference is less than "strong" because it is genuinely possible for the conclusion to be false even if the reason be true. For example, even given his beliefs, Matisse might have, on occasion, released a painting prior to giving it every possible effort, if other motivations or temptations (such as a need for income, or a momentary impulse to please someone) outweighed this conviction. (People do sometimes fail to act in accordance with their deepest convictions.) On the other hand, the degree of validity seems higher than "weak." Although truth of the reason would not establish the truth of the conclusion beyond a reasonable doubt, it would make the truth of the conclusion "a good bet."[1] This step of inference thus receives a rating of "moderate." Notice, incidentally, the use of the square brackets to clarify both the reference of the pronoun "I" in the original discourse and the tense of the verb.

"Don't know" is written beside the statement "Matisse was convinced that an artist can have no greater enemies than his bad paintings," because I lack adequate grounds in order to say that I know that this statement is true. Even if I had heard Matisse himself say so on the radio, in order to say that I know that it is true, I would need to have more contact with him, in which, for example, I could hear him respond at greater length to further questions, or even be acquainted with him and and watch him over a period of time. In the present case, I am in no position to have this knowledge. Even though I did see the English translation of this attributed statement in the book from which it was quoted, it would be a risky to say that therefore I know it to be true. Matisse may have been misquoted, or mistranslated, or quoted out of context, and even if he did actually say this (in French), he may have exaggerated in describing his attitude. More would be needed before I could justifiably say that I really knew that Matisse actually had the conviction described.

Large Complicated Arguments

In any given diagram, some reasons will appear at the top with no arrows above them. As explained previously, these are called the *"basic reasons."* They are the ultimate premises or assumptions on which the reasoning is based. In order for the reasoning in big arguments to be sound, each step of inference (that is, each arrow) needs to be valid and all the relevant basic reasons need to be true. When both conditions are met, the reasoning is sound. Further explanation of how to deal with complex reasoning appears later in this book.

Sometimes, a large diagram with many arrows will have parts that are sound and other parts that are unsound. When this occurs, sometimes it is desirable to go beyond merely evaluating the reasoning and "cut out" and save the parts that are good while trying to replace the unsound parts with slightly different sound steps of reasoning that fit with the good parts and lead to the same final conclusion. Philosophers and other serious thinkers dealing with extremely important problems sometimes test to see whether they can in this way convert partially unsound pieces of reasoning into completely sound arguments.

---

[1] By "a good bet" is meant a wager that one could be relatively confident of winning, but still presenting a small element of risk.

arguments. Their motivation, naturally, is the pursuit of wisdom and knowledge, with all the associated benefits that sound reasoning yields.

Doing the Exercises

In the following exercises, do not be surprised if you find yourself frequently saying "Don't know" when rating the truth or falsity of the reasons. As early Greek philosophers pointed out, true wisdom begins when one realizes how little one really knows. Distinguishing between what one really does, and what one does *not*, know, is worth practicing. In particular, you may write a lot of "Don't know's" in application to statements about events far away in space or time, but in application to matters closer to home, (which are, of course, usually the matters about which reliable reasoning will have the most important immediate personal implications in life), you probably will find that you are able to say "Definitely true" or "Probably true" (or "false") more often. For example, Although I may need to say that I "Don't know" or am "Uncertain" whether an alleged historical event happened a thousand years ago, I certainly can say that it is "Definitely false" that I ate eggs for breakfast this morning, and that it is "Definitely true" that my car started this afternoon when I turned the key. When applying logical methods to situations and problems in your own life where you are personally closer to the relevant facts, you generally will know the truth or falsity of more of the relevant statements, so no serious problem exists here for your use of logic.

Do NOT make the mistake of giving an inference a low rating because it contains unclear language. If you do not know what the statements in an argument are supposed to mean, then you *do not know* whether it is valid or invalid, or sound or unsound. It might be sound, for all you know, as might be recognized once it was clarified. Or it might be unsound, and this might be seen once it was clarified. Unclear reasoning cannot be rated for soundness at all until the language is clarified. So, clarify it *first*, if necessary, with footnotes [or square brackets], and *then* evaluate it.

EXERCISES 1A

INSTRUCTIONS: For each instance of reasoning diagrammed in the exercises on the following pages:

(*i*) Express what you know (or do not know) about the truth or falsity of each basic reason by circling it and writing either "definitely true," "probably true," "uncertain/don't know," "probably false," or "definitely false" by the end of the lasso.

(*ii*) Rate the degree of confirmation (or "degree of validity") of each separate step of inference in the diagram, writing either "nil," "weak," "moderate," "can't tell," "strong," or "deductively valid" BESIDE EACH ARROW, according to how you rate the inference.

(*iii*) Judge the soundness of each step of inference, writing either "sound," "probably sound," "marginal," "can't say," "probably unsound," or "unsound," according to your verdict.

You may convey your answers in *either* of the following two ways:

(1) On a copying machine, or by hand, make a copy of the diagrams in the exercises and (*i*) indicate what you know (or do not know) about the truth or falsity of each reason beside a circle around that reason, (*ii*) write the validity rating alongside each arrow in each diagram, and, (*iii*) write your soundness verdict below the diagram prefaced with "Verdict," as illustrated in the examples in the text.
Or alternatively, if you prefer,
(2) On a separate sheet of paper, alongside a number corresponding to each exercise, you may indicate (*i*) what you know (or do not know) regarding the truth or falsity of each reason, (*ii*) write the degree of confirmation (that is, degree of validity) of the inference, and (*iii*) give your verdict regarding soundness. Thus, for example, expressed in this format, one student's complete evaluation of one exercise argument might read like this:

(*i*) Definitely true
(*ii*) weak
(*iii*) unsound

A-1. Dana is very good-looking. Therefore, Dana will, in general, be a reliable, dependable person.

> Dana is very good-looking.
>
> ↓
>
> Dana will, in general, be a
> reliable, dependable person.

A-2. John owns an automobile. So, John owns a car, truck, van, dune buggy, motorhome, or dragster.

> John owns an automobile.
>
> ↓
>
> John owns a car, truck, van, dune
> buggy, motorhome, or dragster.

From a Lee Two-stage Maxifilter radio commercial:

A-3. . . . If the engine is the most important part of a car, then the oil filter must be the second most important part, since the oil filter protects the engine.

> The oil filter protects the engine.
>
> ↓
>
> If the engine is the most important part of a car, then the oil filter [is] the second most important part.

A-4. She never will speak to him again. Therefore, she will not speak to him next week.

> She never will speak to him again.
>
> ↓
>
> She will not speak to him next week.

A-5. She said that she will never speak to him again. Therefore, she will not speak to him next week.

> She said that she will never
> speak to him again.
>
> ↓
>
> She will not speak to him
> next week.

A-6. A lot of "Incompletes" on a student's college grade transcript, even if these incompletes are shown as having later been made up, may raise questions about a student's work habits and look bad to some readers. So, students who care about the appearance of their college grade record should try to keep their "Incompletes" to a reasonable minimum.

> A lot of "Incompletes" on a student's
> college grade transcript, even if these
> incompletes are shown as having later
> been made up, may raise questions about
> a student's work habits and look bad to
> some readers.
>
> ↓
>
> Students who care about the
> appearance of their college grade
> record should try to keep their
> "Incompletes" to a reasonable
> minimum.

A-7. According to a recent article in the highly prestigious journal *Philosophical Review*, Saint Anselm's attempted proof of the existence of God is sound. Therefore, Anselm's proof is sound.

> According to a recent article in the highly prestigious journal, *Philosophical Review*, Saint Anselm's attempted proof of the existence of God is sound.
>
> ↓
>
> Anselm's proof is sound.

From Don Thomas, "Nature of Things: Wildlife Facts," *The Moneysaver* , p. 13:

A-8. Some birds that migrate thousands of miles each year have an incredible capacity to hear low sounds. For example, some birds are directed toward their destination by the sound of an ocean's low rumble on surf 100 miles away.

> Some birds [that migrate thousands of miles each year] are directed toward their destination by the sound of an ocean's low rumble on surf 100 miles away.
>
> ↓
>
> Some birds that migrate thousands of miles each year have an incredible ability to hear low sounds.

A-9. In highway motorcycle accidents, there is a significant danger of the rider sustaining serious injury. For this reason, motorcycle riders who value their health should employ whatever reasonable, genuinely effective safety measures they can.

> In highway motorcycle accidents, there is a significant danger of the rider sustaining serious injury.
>
> ↓
>
> Motorcycle riders who value their health should employ whatever reasonable, genuinely effective safety measures they can.

A-10. Bob's stockbroker has always been right in his past six predictions of stock price changes that he has made to Bob over the past year. Therefore, he is right in his current prediction that the stock he mentioned will soon increase in value.

> Bob's stockbroker has always been right in his past six predictions of stock price changes that he has made to Bob over the past year.
>
> ↓
>
> He is right in his current prediction that the stock he mentioned will soon increase in value.

How to Analyze and Diagram One-premise Arguments

In the previous exercises, a number of short discourses[1] containing reasoning, and immediately thereafter, a diagram of the reasoning were given to you already completed. But in real life, diagrams are seldom given already completed. Instead, you are given only a discourse containing reasoning in more or less unclear form, and *you* must figure out what the reasoning is supposed to be and determine its reliability, often quickly in your mind. This valuable ability can be developed by diagramming the reasoning in argued discourses given in discourse form, and then evaluating the diagrams. But before practicing this on the next exercises, here are some crucial things you need to know:

A **"reason"** is any statement given in support, justification, or explanation of some fact, claim, expectation, prediction, or assertion.[2] Sometimes the reasons given actually explain or justify such claims or expectations, and sometimes they do not, but in either case they still are called "reasons." The statements that someone tries to support or explain by reasons in a discourse are called **"conclusions."** In applying the term "conclusion," we will consider only the writer's or speaker's apparent intentions; whether or not the conclusion is *actually* supported by the reasons given will not matter to *this* term's application (as it does to the application of terms like "valid," "invalid," "sound," and "unsound"). Thus, for example, we may say of an author, "His conclusion is not justified by his reasons."

Using the words "reason" and "conclusion," **"reasoning"** may be defined as *any discourse in which some statement is given as a reason for some conclusion.* To accept some claim as true on the basis of supporting reasons, or to offer, or consider, reasons in support or explanation of something, is to engage in reasoning. If the *purpose or intent* of the reasoning is to support, justify, or prove a conclusion, it is said to contain "argument," or to be "an argument." Arguments, then, contain reasoning.

The presence of reasoning is often (but not always!) signalled, in the English language, by certain special words called "inference indicators." One important group of inference indicators often indicate that the statement or clause following them is a "conclusion" — in other words, that it is alleged to be supported by some other statement(s) *that are given elsewhere in the same discourse.* The words in the following list indicate that what they precede is a "conclusion":

---

[1] A "discourse" is a sentence or series of sentences in one or more paragraphs.

[2] Readers acquainted with formal deductive logic will perceive that the concept of a "reason" used in Direct Natural Logic® is similar to the concept of a "premise" as this term is used in deductive logic, but has a wider extension. The premises of a deductively valid argument are one species of reason, but other kinds of inference also involve "reasons."

Partial list of words or phrases that often function as inference indicators PRECEDING CONCLUSIONS

consequently . . .

therefore . . .

which shows that . . .

proves that . . .

hence . . .

so . . .

you see that . . .

implies that . . .

entails that . . .

accordingly . . .

it must be that . . .

I conclude that . . .

for this reason, . . .

points to the conclusion that . .

allows us to infer that . . .

suggests very strongly that . . .

leads me to believe that . . .

bears out the point that . . .

thus . . . (frequent exceptions)

demonstrates that . . .

it follows that . . .

in this way one sees that . . .

then . . . (without preceding 'if';

    has exceptions)

These words generally, but not always, indicate that the statement following them is a conclusion. Notice that in order to be a "conclusion" in the sense in which this term is used here, *the reasons(s) alleged to justify the conclusion must actually be stated, and be present, in the discourse.*

As mentioned earlier, statements given as justifying or explaining a conclusion are called "reasons" (or sometimes, "premises"). The English language has another group of special words that do the job of indicating that the statement or clause that follows them is being given as a reason for something said elsewhere in the same discourse. Here are some common "reason indicator words":

Partial list of words or phrases that often function as inference indicators PRECEDING REASONS

as . . .(many exceptions)

since . . . (many exceptions)

for . . . (many exceptions)

because . . .

as shown by . . .

as indicated by . . .

follows from . . .

being that . . .

being as . . .

inasmuch as . . .

in the first place . . .

firstly . . .

seeing that . . .

for the reasons that . . .

in view of the fact that . . .

on the correct supposition that .

assuming, as we may, that . . .

may be inferred from . . .

may be deduced from . . .

may be derived from . . .

whereas . . . (in legal

    documents)

in the second place . . .

secondly . . .

The words in this second list are also "inference indicator words." They indicate that what follows them is a reason or premise.

Writers and speakers sometimes present arguments carefully, with each individual reason or conclusion precisely expressed in its own separate sentence, and with all steps of reasoning clearly marked by inference indicator words. You have encountered some examples of such discourses in examples and exercises previously. But usually discourses containing reasoning are not so well-organized and clearly written, so one must learn to extract the reasoning from them sensitively and thoughtfully.

Help in Recognizing Reasoning

Here are some pointers:

A. *The presence of a word or phrase from either of the lists of inference indicators given earlier is a good clue that a discourse contains reasoning, but there are many exceptions.* The word "since," for example, is often used to express a relationship in time rather than a logical relationship. Contrase the following examples. In the first discourse, the word "since" means "because" or "inasmuch as," and signals reasoning. In the second, "since" functions as a temporal word, rather than as an inference indicator, and no reasoning is involved.

It should be considered armed robbery since he carried a gun. *(Argument)*

It has been five years since he carried a gun. *(Not argument)*

Another example is the word "as," which is often used to express comparisons (for instance, "He can run as well as John"). Many of the other listed words can also perform other linguistic jobs. For example, the word "for" is frequently used as a preposition (as in "she used a newspaper for a sunshade"). In such cases, they do not indicate reasoning.

In trying to determine whether a discourse contains argument, there are other possible sources of difficulty:

B. *Sometimes reason(s) or premise(s) come before the conclusion in a discourse, and sometimes they follow.* There is no fixed order in which reasons and conclusions come in discourses. They can come in any order. If any inference indicator words are present, use them to identify the conclusion(s) and reason(s).

C. *Some reasoned discourses contain NO inference-indicator words.* For example:

The Vietnam war was wrong. You should have opposed it.

Although no inference indicator is present, the first statement presumably gives the speaker's reason for the second statement. Nothing makes this explicit, but the fact that one could insert the word "therefore" between the two sentences without changing the sense of the discourse shows that this reading is reasonable.

When you encounter a discourse that contains no inference indicator words but that may nevertheless contain reasoning, stop and consider very carefully whether such an interpretation is really justifiable. Do not go overboard and think you see reasoning in every passage you read. When attributing reasoning to discourses in which inference indicators or other explicit signals of reasoning are absent, proceed very cautiously and conservatively. A good rule to follow is the **"Principle of Charity."** In general, the Principle of Charity says : **When analyzing reasoning, always analyze it in the way that interprets it as the strongest possible reasoning compatible with the inference indicators in the discourse.** That is, when the language of a given discourse leaves its logical structure, or nature, open to various interpretations, choose the interpretation that results in the soundest possible reasoning — that is, choose the strongest or logically best (rather than a weaker or logically inferior) interpretation of it.

This principle has two important consequences, which can be roughly stated as follows: (1) Given a choice between categorizing a discourse as "bad reasoning" or "nonreasoning," categorize it as the second (nonreasoning). (2) If a discourse contains reasoning and you must choose between several different interpretations or analyses (diagrams) of the reasoning, choose the one that results in the strongest reasoning. Here is what this means:

First, if a given discourse contains no inference indicators or other definite signs of reasoning, and if the only reasoning that could possibly be attributed to it would be obviously illogical, then categorize the discourse as nonreasoning. So, if it is unclear whether an author is giving reasons for a conclusion at all, and if the only reasoning you can attribute makes no sense logically, then do not attribute any reasoning at all. (Notice that the Principle of Charity does not prevent you from criticizing such a discourse because it contains no logical reasoning.) So, if a statement in a discourse would not follow logically from some other statement(s) in the discourse, do *not* interpret that statement as a conclusion supposedly supported or explained by those other statements unless the author has explicitly indicated that this statement is supposed to be supported or explained by the other(s).

The second consequence of the Principle makes sense not merely in terms of kindness and fairness, to authors (because we only attribute bad reasoning to them when they are clearly guilty of it), but also in terms of our own personal self-interest. Speaking at least for myself: *The main value of logic is not so much in refuting other people's arguments as it is in finding the truth through reasoning.* This priority justifies the Principle of Charity. For whenever one interprets an argument in a way that makes it appear weak and worthless when actually it would have been strong and sound if interpreted another way, one may overlook, and fail to obtain, a priceless treasure — namely, the opportunity to learn a new truth, with all its accompanying benefits. This consideration also justifies the first consequence of the general principle: if a discourse contains neither a structure that indicates reasoning, nor any inference indicator phrase, and if no statement in the discourse can serve even as even a somewhat plausible reason for any other, then do *not* regard or categorize the discourse as containing reasoning. There is no point in going to extremes to "find" reasoning in a discourse when already you can see that in your next step, when the reasoning is evaluated, you will reject and discard it as worthless. That wastes time and energy. Remember, however, that when an inference indicator explicitly appears and/or the author clearly intends an argument, then the discourse is categorized as "reasoning" *even if* it is defective reasoning.

When no inference indicator word is present in a discourse, how can one tell whether the discourse contains reasoning or not? And if it contains reasoning, how can one tell which statements express reasons and which express conclusions? This is done by paying close attention to the *content* of the statements to see whether any transference of belief, or acceptance, between statements is justified or suggested by what the statements say.[1] Consider, for example, the following discourse:

> That exhaust pipe is very hot, so you should not touch it with your bare hands.

A step of reasoning takes place when a belief in the first statement ("that exhaust pipe is very hot") leads one to believe the second ("you should not touch it with your bare hands"). The content of these statements would be sufficient to justify this transfer of belief even if no inference indicator were present so that it read as follows:

> That exhaust pipe is very hot. You should not touch it with your bare hands.

---

[1] This formulation is due to Edward Regis, Jr.

In discourses that do *not* contain reasoning, in contrast, no such transference of belief from statement to statement is suggested or justified. For example:

> In June 1970, a group of young couples joined in a symposium in St. Louis. They were all in their mid or late twenties and had been married for less than two years. The group was made up of teachers, lawyers, doctors, and skilled craftspeople.

All of these statements relate to the same topic, but each statement reports a separate fact and none of these statements should cause one to believe any of the others. Because no transference of belief among the statements in this discourse is justified or intended, no step of reasoning exists here.

If some statement in a discourse is clearly intended to cause the reader or hearer to believe another statement in the discourse, then the discourse contains the one statement as a *reason* and the other statement as a *conclusion,* even if the discourse contains no inference indicator word. But if *no* transference of belief is justified or intended, then categorize the discourse as nonargument.

D.   *Entire arguments, including both reasons and conclusions, may be contained in a single sentence.* Consider this example:

> Since we cannot live well and be happy unless our future is secure, and such security is impossible without knowledge, and obtaining knowledge requires sound reasoning, it is obvious that sound reasoning is necessary for living well and being happy.

Replacing the inference indicator "since" with a simple "therefore" and rewriting the discourse using individual sentences that separate the conclusion from the reasons, we get:

1. We cannot live well and be happy unless our future is secure.
2. Such security is impossible without knowledge.
3. Obtaining knowledge requires sound reasoning.
4. Therefore, sound reasoning is necessary for living well and being happy.

E. *Modal words or phrases (like "must," "cannot," etc.) expressing necessity or impossibility sometimes are used as inference indicators to signal reasoning or argument.*

Determining the Direction of the Reasoning

When reasoning is detected, one must determine its *direction*. To do this, one must determine which statements in the discourse are given as *reasons* for other statements and which statements are *conclusions* drawn from other statements. (Remember that any statement given in support of another is called a "reason," whether it is a good reason or not, and any statement that an someone presents as justified by some reason in a discourse is termed a "conclusion," whether or not the reason really supports or explains it.)

Inference indicators, like those listed in the previous pages, help one make this determination. The appearance of any from the *first* group generally indicates that the statement that follows is a *conclusion*. And the appearance of any from the *second* group normally signals that the statement that follows it is a *reason*.

Subtle differences of meaning exist, of course, among the indicators within each group. To say that a certain reason "proves" a certain conclusion, for example, sounds stronger and more assertive than to say that it "leads me to believe" this conclusion. But for present logical purposes, this difference is not important.[1] Since we are interested only in the justificatory or explanatory relationships among statements, whenever any of those inference-indicator words appears, we will simply replace it with a uniform 'therefore' and rewrite the discourse as follows:

Reason

therefore

Conclusion

For convenience, the word 'therefore' is replaced with an arrow:

Reason

Conclusion

Diagrams like this are called **"arrow diagrams."** The arrow (which is read as "therefore") is always drawn pointing toward a conclusion. Remember that the

---

[1] *Note to Advanced Readers:* Some introductory textbooks teach that the choice of inference indicator word determines whether the reasoning is "deductive" or "inductive." According to Moore & Parker, Copi, etc., for example, when strong-sounding inference indicators (like "proves conclusively") are used, the reasoning is "deductive,"whereas when less assertive indicators (like "shows") are used, the reasoning is "inductive." This remarkabledoctrine entails that it is unnecessary to consider the content of the statements themselves to determine the type of reasoning constituted. Although these texts repeat and distinguish the two lists of indicators found in *PRNL* (1973), naturally they cannot specifically ennumerate which are "deduction-indicators" versus "induction-indicators."

arrow represents an inference of any kind, a step of passing *from* some fact or statement (the reason) *to* another fact or statement (the conclusion) All of the different kinds of reasoning or logical inference that exist[1] will be represented by this universal symbol.

The fact that the arrow is drawn pointing downward is purely conventional. We could construct our diagrams with arrows pointing upwards or sideways:

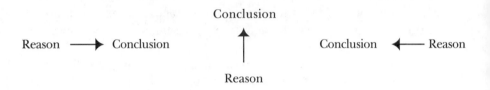

But we will draw the arrow pointing downward. (Do not make the silly reviewer's mistake of thinking that because the arrows are pointing downwards, all the inferences are "deductions.")

EXERCISES 1B

For each argument in the exercises on this page and the next, (1) make a diagram with a arrow pointing from the reason (or premise) to the conclusion. That is, use the inference indicator word or phrase (plus common sense) to decide which statement is the reason and which statement is the conclusion, and then write down the reason(s), draw an arrow pointing downward, and write down the conclusion.

Next, after diagramming the reasoning, evaluate the argument fully exactly as in the previous group of exercises (which were given already diagrammed). (2) Circle the reason (or premise) and write what you know or do not know about its truth or falsity. (3) Rate the degree of validity of the step of inference. And finally, (4) give a verdict about its soundness or reliability.

B-1. This dentist, Dr. Jones, has a beautiful, well-decorated waiting room and office. I conclude from this that he does good dental work.

B-2. It is good to be able to avoid being deceived by unsound reasoning, because unsound reasoning can lead people into unwise actions that they will later regret, or prevent them from choosing the best courses of action available.

---

[1]*Note to Advanced Readers:* These include "deductions," "inductions," "conductions," explanations, postulations, predictions, justifications, semantic inferences, modal inferences, etc.

B-3. The new T-car built by the Economy Motorcar Company gets more than twice as many kilometers per liter of gasoline as George's present car does. For this reason, if George trades his present car in for a T-car, his total cost to own and operate this new car over the next five years will be lower than they would be if he kept his present car.

Adapted from H. L. Mencken, *The Vintage Mencken:*
B-4. Usually, in the past, roses have smelled better to you than cabbages. Therefore, soup made from roses will taste better to you than soup made from cabbage.
Special instruction: Take "you" here to refer to yourself, the student doing this exercise.

Adapted from Rene Descartes, *Meditations:*
B-5. I am thinking at this moment. Therefore, I exist at this moment.
Special instruction: Take the pronoun "I" here to refer to you yourself, the student doing this exercise (and not to Descartes or anyone else).

From a Law School Admission Test Study Guide:
B-6. Since all rabbits that I have seen have short tails, all rabbits have short tails.
Special instruction: Use the pronoun "I' when making the diagram, and when you evaluate the reasoning, take "I" to refer to yourself personally, the student doing this exercise.

From Robert Morison, "Where is Biology Taking Us?," *Science*, 155 (1967), 429-33:
B-7. There are several reasons for believing that we [cannot] keep our system of moral values and our system of scientific expertise in separate water-tight compartments. Perhaps most important is the fact that science, and especially biological science, has produced evidence to reinforce some ancient exhortations and weaken the hold of others, and has invented, or at least called attention to the significance of, an entirely new range of good and bad behavior.
Special instruction: Trim away the extra words at the beginning of both the statement of the reason and also of the conclusion.

2

Conditional Relationships

Statements of the form:

> If A, then B.

are called **"conditional statements."** A conditional statement has an *antecedent clause* and a *consequent clause*. In the above example, the letter "A" stands in place of the antecedent clause, and the letter "B" stands in place of the consequent clause. Each conditional statement says that in case the situation described by its antecedent clause exists, then so too exists (or will exist) the situation described by its consequent clause. For example, the conditional statement,

> If it rains today, then we will get wet.

says that in the event of rain today (an event satisfying the description in the antecedent clause), another event (described by the consequent clause) also will occur — namely, our getting wet. In conditional statements, the word "then" frequently is omitted, and the word "if" is left to do the entire job by itself. For example,

> If it rains today, we will get wet.

This sentence conveys the same meaning as the sentence in the previous example containing the word "then." Sometimes, the antecedent clause appears AFTER the consequent clause (as in "We will get wet, if it rains today")

Some conditional statements are true, and other conditional statements are false. If the universe is such that the antecedent clause cannot come (or be) true without the consequent clause also becoming (or being) true, then the entire conditional statement is true. Here are two examples of *true* conditional statements:

If Bob weighs more than 80 kg., then he weighs more than 75 kg.

If hydrogen is burned in the atmosphere, then some water vapor is
produced.

On the other hand, if the antecedent clause of a conditional is true (or becomes
true), but the consequent clause is false (or does not become true), then the
whole conditional statement is false. Here are two examples of false (or untrue)
conditional statements:

If the fuel tank of my car is filled with water instead of gasoline,
then my car will still continue to run OK.

If butter is frozen, it turns to gold.

In these examples, if the situation described by the antecedent clause of these
conditionals gets fulfilled, the situation described by the consequent still will *not*
come to pass, so these conditional statements "break their promise" and are
false. Notice that false conditional statements are still conditional statements;
they are conditional statements that are false.

In logic, conditional statements are also often called simply "conditionals"
or "hypotheticals" for short, and this terminology will be used here too.

Conditional statements often play crucial roles in extremely important
reasoning, so it is important to know how to operate with them. Some patterns of
inference involving conditionals are difficult to understand or evaluate without
special training in logic, which is provided here. It helps to begin by understanding the concept of "necessary conditions" and the concept of "sufficient
conditions." These two concepts will be explained separately, and then compared
and contrasted.

1. Necessary and Sufficient Conditions

A **sufficient condition** for some situation is any circumstance or condition
whose existence or fulfillment, by itself, is, or would be, enough to bring about,
or guarantee the existence of, that situation. For example, heating a
combustible material to its kindling point in the presence of oxygen is a
sufficient condition for the occurrence of burning or combustion; having a wife is
a sufficient condition for being married; and owning a motorcycle is a sufficient
condition for owning a motor vehicle.

In general, if *A* is a sufficient condition for *B*, then a conditional with a
description of *A* as its antecedent and a description of *B* as its consequent will be
true:

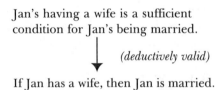

(A) is a sufficient condition for (B).

(deductively valid)

If A, then B.

So, for example, in the illustration about having a wife, the following inference is deductively valid:

Jan's having a wife is a sufficient
condition for Jan's being married.

(deductively valid)

If Jan has a wife, then Jan is married.

Likewise, in general, with the following two ways of talking,

1. (*A*) is a sufficient condition for (*B*).
2. If *A*, then *B*.

one can always replace the first with the second, or reason from the first to the second with deductive validity.

On the other hand, a **necessary condition** for some situation is any circumstance or condition that needs to be fulfilled in order for that situation to exist. For example, being female is a necessary condition for being a wife. And a necessary condition for the occurrence of burning is the presence of oxygen (which means that without oxygen, combustion will not occur). Notice that the presence of oxygen is not itself a sufficient condition for the occurrence of burning — oxygen can be present without combustion taking place, for example when the temperature is below the kindling point, or there is no fuel. A necessary condition does not need to be a sufficient condition — that is, a necessary condition is not required to be enough, by itself, to guarantee that the specified condition exist. A necessary condition can be simply one of the requirements that needs to be satisfied for the situation to come about — for example, being female is a necessary, but not a sufficient, condition for being a wife.

Notice, too, that one may speak of necessary conditions (and also, of sufficient conditions) in reference to situations that do not involve relations of cause and effect. For example, a necessary condition for a number's being less than 10 is that it be less than 12. A necessary condition for being a mammal is being warm-blooded. A necessary condition for being a mother (in the biological sense) is that one be a parent. A necessary condition for reasoning to be "sound" is that it be "valid." And so on.

Notice also that not only can something be a necessary condition without being a sufficient condition (as the presence of fuel is necessary, but not sufficient, for burning, and validity is necessary, but not sufficient, for the soundness of reasoning), but also something can be a sufficient condition without being a necessary condition (for example, owning a Rolls Royce limousine is a sufficient, but not a necessary, condition for owning a motor

When the statement of a necessary condition, or of a sufficient condition, is made, naturally it is important that the context be clearly stated or understood. For example, you have probably heard about the proverbial "straw that broke the camel's back." Suppose someone is about to put that "last straw" on the back of a heavily loaded camel and you say, "Adding that straw will be a sufficient condition to break the camel's back" or "If that straw is put on its back, then its back will break." What you probably mean is that putting that straw on its back in the present circumstances (with the camel under its present heavy load) would be sufficient to break its back. You probably do not mean that in general, at any time, whether loaded or unloaded, putting that straw on its back would be sufficient to break it.

Necessary conditions also are expressible using conditional statements. Assume that the presence of oxygen is a necessary condition for the burning of a fire; then if a fire is burning, what must be the case with regard to the presence of oxygen? (Stop and try to figure out the answer before reading on.) The answer is that in that case, oxygen must be present, since without oxygen, fire will not burn (because, the presence of oxygen is a necessary condition for a fire to burn). In other words, the following reasoning is deductively valid:

> The presence of oxygen is a necessary
> condition for the burning of a fire.
>
> $\downarrow$ *(deductively valid)*
>
> If a fire is burning, then oxygen is present.

The same holds true in general. Suppose, abstractly, that Y is a necessary condition for X. Then if X comes about or exists, what must be the case with regard to Y? Stop and try to figure out the answer before reading on. Remember that we are supposing that Y is a necessary condition for X. The answer is that Y also must have come about or been the case, since without Y, X would not have happened (because, by assumption, Y is a necessary condition for X). In other words,

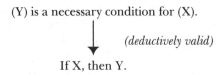

(Y) is a necessary condition for (X).

(deductively valid)

If X, then Y.

So, too, in general, with the following two ways of talking,

1. (*Y*) is a necessary condition for (*X*).
2. If *X*, then *Y*.

one always can validly replace the first with the second, or reason from the first to the second with deductive validity.

The "Only If" Conditional Form

Other language besides the familiar "if . . . , then _ _ _ " can be used to express conditional statements. For example, if the presence of oxygen is a necessary condition for the occurrence of burning, then burning will occur only if oxygen is present.

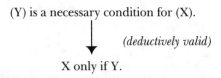

The presence of oxygen is a necessary
condition for the occurrence of burning.

(deductively valid)

Burning occurs only if oxygen is present.

Likewise in general,

(Y) is a necessary condition for (X).

(deductively valid)

X only if Y.

Actually, "*X* only if *Y*" is just another way of saying "If *X*, then *Y*." The two ways of expressing a conditional

1. A only if B.
2. If A, then B.

say the same thing, and either may at any time be inferred from the other with deductive validity. For example,

A fire is burning only if oxygen is present.

(deductively valid)

If a fire is burning, then oxygen is present.

One also can pass from a conditional of the second form to a conditional like the first with deductive validity:

If a fire is burning, then oxygen is present.

(deductively valid)

A fire is burning only if oxygen is present.

In general, it is always valid to pass from a conditional of the one form to a conditional of the other form:

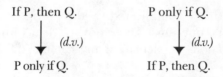

If P, then Q.   P only if Q.

(d.v.)   *(d.v.)*

P only if Q.   If P, then Q.

The two forms of the conditional are equivalent, and either can, at any time, be used in place of the other. This fact sometimes baffles and confuses people, probably because in this way of expressing a conditional statement:

ANTECEDENT only if *CONSEQUENT.*

the little word "if" *precedes the consequent,* whereas in the "if . . . , then _ _ _ " formulation, the "if" *precedes the antecedent.* Remember that when the word "only" is placed in front of the word "if," it completely turns its meaning around and makes the clause that follows the "if" be the consequent rather than the antecedent of the conditional statement.

2. Other Forms of Conditional Statements

Some additional important facts that you should know about conditional statements are:

1. Saying *"R, if B"* is equivalent to saying *"If B, then R."* B is in the antecedent position in both versions.

2. To assert *BOTH* that (B) is a sufficient condition for (R) AND that (B) is a necessary condition for (R) — On those rare occasions when both are true —

one says:

$$R \text{ if and only if } B,$$

which is merely a short way of saying, "*R*, if *B*" *and* "*R* only if *B*." It means that whenever *R* is true, so too is *B*, and whenever *B* is true, so too is *R*. "*R* if and only if *B*" is equivalent to "*B* if and only if *R*." For example, "It is a rabbit if it is a bunny" *(R*, if *B)* plus "It is a rabbit only if it is a bunny" *(R* only if *B)* entails "It is a rabbit if and only if it is a bunny," which is equivalent to "It is a bunny if and only if it is a rabbit." A statement of this form is called a "biconditional," because it is really two conditionals joined together.

     3. Sentences containing the word "when" often do the same job as conditionals. "If *P*, then *Q*" follows logically from the statement "When *P*, then *Q*," for example.

Negation

     To understand more complicated valid patterns of reasoning involving conditional statements, one must know how to deal with the "negations" of statements. The "negation" or "denial" of any statement, for example,

     I. The house is warm.

can be formed by inserting the word "not," or words that have the same meaning, into the original sentence — as, for example,

     II. The house is *not* warm.
           The house is*n't* warm.
           It is not the case that the house is warm.

The sentences in group *II* are called "negations" or "denials" of the sentence in group *I*. If the sentences in group *II* are true, then the sentence in group *I* is false. And if (*I*) "The house is warm" is true, then all the sentences in group *II* are false. (It is a fundamental law of logic that it *never* can happen that *both* a sentence *and* its negation are true.) For short, later in this section,

     "Not-*P*" abbreviates "It is not the case that *P*."

(where "*P*" here is a letter standing in place of any sentence).

     If the negation of a sentence is itself negated, the result is called a "double negation." For instance, "It is not the case that it is not the case that *P*," or for short, "Not-not-*P*. In a double negation, the two negations cancel each other, and the result is equivalent to a positive assertion of the unnegated sentence. For example, the double negation, "It is not the case that Jill is not late," is simply equivalent to the statement "Jill is late."[1]

3. Pure Hypothetical Syllogisms

The deductively valid step of inference called a "(**pure**) **hypothetical syllogism**" occurs when the antecedent of one conditional is the same as the consequent of another conditional and these two conditionals are put together in a pattern to lead to a third conditional statement as a conclusion, like this:

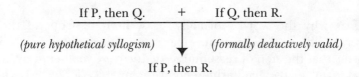

If P, then Q.   +   If Q, then R.

(pure hypothetical syllogism)   *(formally deductively valid)*

If P, then R.

The deductive validity of such reasoning is obvious. For, suppose that "*P*" (which is the antecedent of the conditional in the conclusion below the arrow) happens to be true. What, in that event, must be the case regarding the consequent, "*R*," of the same conditional? Well, *together with* the conditional on the *top left* in the premises, the supposition that "*P*" is true would logically entail that "*Q*" also is true. And from "*Q*" together with the conditional on the *top right* in the diagram, it would follow logically that "*R*" is true. So, taken together, the two conditionals in the reasons logically entail that if "*P*" is true, then "*R*" also is true. In other words, the conclusion follows from them that "if *P*, then *R*" — which is the drawn conclusion.

Pure hypothetical syllogisms are also deductively valid when the clauses in the premises contain negative terms, or negations of statements (as long as the consequent of one conditional is identical to the antecedent of the other conditional and the reasoning has the pattern shown). No matter what meaningful sentences are substituted for the letters "*P*," "*Q*," and "*R*," the resulting *pure hypothetical syllogism* is deductively valid simply in virtue of the statements having the logical form shown in the outline diagram. For example, the following is a deductively valid pure hypothetical syllogism:

---

[1]Some philosophical logicians (the "Intuitionists" among the philosophers of mathematics, for example) do refuse to accept such equivalences in the special case of "nonconstructive" mathematical proofs in certain cases involving infinity, but this advanced topic in the philosophy of mathematics is beyond the purview of an elementary introductory logic textbook, and in any case, for our purposes, will be no problem.

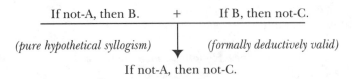

If not-A, then B.   +   If B, then not-C.

(pure hypothetical syllogism)   *(formally deductively valid)*

If not-A, then not-C.

It also would have been valid if "not-not-C" had been put in the places where "not-C" is shown here, or if other negative statements had been substituted for "*P*," "*Q*," and "*R*" in the original schematic form. The result will be deductively valid purely because it has this pattern or "*logical form.*"

This is why the word "formally" is written in front of the phrase "deductively valid" in the diagram. The rating "formally deductively valid" simply means that the step of reasoning is deductively valid entirely because of the "logical form" or pattern of the sentences alone. *CAUTION:* Do not make the mistake of automatically categorizing an inference as "not deductively valid" or "deductively invalid" because it does not correspond to a valid logical form. This error, which is made in many defective logic textbooks, is called "*the formalization fallacy.*" Remember that reasoning that is not *formally* deductively valid can be, and often is, still deductively valid through the *meanings* of words like "suitcases," "luggage," "automobile," "car," "bachelor," "unmarried," etc. as well as other factors, as we saw in previous illustrations and exercise sets. Reasoning that is not an instance of a deductively valid logical form is properly evaluated by the "magic question" method presented earlier.

Transposition ("Contraposition")

Another important deductively valid step of reasoning with conditional statements is called **"transposition,"** or sometimes "*contraposition.*"[1] In this pattern, one starts with a conditional statement, say,

(A)   If *P*, then *Q*.

and infers from it another conditional whose antecedent is a negation of the original's consequent, and whose consequent is a negation of the original's

---

[1]Many logicians restrict the term "transposition" to the replacement of sentence forms like "If *P*, then *Q*" with the equivalent form "If not-*Q*, then not-*P*," and apply the term "contraposition" only to inferences between corresponding conditionals that involve quantificational terms like "all" — as for example, from "All *F*'s are *G*'s" to "All non-*G*'s are non-*F*'s."

antecedent, like this:

(B)   If not *Q,* then not *P.*

I will call conditionals of the forms **(A)** and **(B)** "transpositive forms" or "transpositives" of each other. For example, the transpositive of

(A) If Jones is ill, then Smith is away.

is

(B) If Smith is not away, then Jones is not ill.

Conditional **(A)** is the transpositive of conditional **(B)**, and conditional **(B)** is the transpositive of conditional **(A)**.

    A highly useful step of deductively valid reasoning consists in going from a conditional statement to its transpositive form. Unlike most inferences in natural language, this is another rare case in which the validity of the inference is due entirely to the pattern in which a few crucial words (like "if-then" and "not") appear in the statements, and does not depend on the meaning or semantic content of the rest of the words (so long as they make sense). Here is the logical form of the inference:

(A)   If P, then Q.

(transposition)   ↓   *(formally deductively valid)*

(B)   If not Q, then not P.

Here is an example of an inference having this pattern:

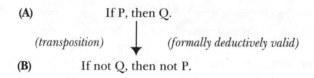

If this car belongs to Henry, then it has blue upholstery.

(transposition)   ↓   *(formally deductively valid)*

If this car does not have blue upholstery, then it does not belong to Henry.

Conditional **(B)** is the transpositive form of conditional **(A)**. **(A)** is also equivalent to the transpositive of **(B)**, because if we apply transposition to **(B)**, the double negatives "cancel out," resulting in **(A)**:

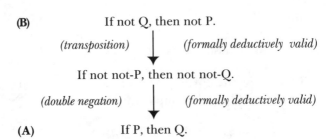

(B)   If not Q, then not P.

   (transposition)   *(formally deductively valid)*

               If not not-P, then not not-Q.

   (double negation)   *(formally deductively valid)*

(A)   If P, then Q.

This is also one of those unusual cases in which the inference is, or would be, deductively valid going in either direction — from **(A)** to **(B)**, or from **(B)** to **(A)**. Hence, replacing a conditional by its transpositive form, or passing from a conditional to its transpositive form, is always deductively valid reasoning. If a conditional statement is true, so too always is its transpositive form.

<h3 style="text-align:center">T R A N S P O S I T I O N</h3>

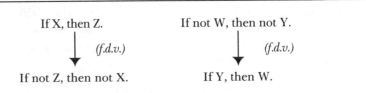

If X, then Z.   If not W, then not Y.

   (f.d.v.)   *(f.d.v.)*

If not Z, then not X.   If Y, then W.

The rule of inference of transposition can also be stated in words as follows:

TRANSPOSITION: *Given the statement of a conditional, it is deductively valid to infer the truth of another conditional statement that has as its antecedent the negation of the first conditional's consequent, and that has as its consequent the negation of the first conditional's antecedent.*

When the consequent of a conditional expresses a necessary condition for its antecedent, the deductive validity of such inferences is especially obvious. For example, suppose that Q is a necessary condition for P, so that

(X)   If *P*, then *Q*.

It follows that if *Q* is not the case, then neither is *P*:

(Y)   If not *Q*, then not *P*.

And going in the other direction, conditional **(Y)**, "If not *Q*, then not *P*" implies that (*Q*) is a necessary condition for (*P*), which, as discussed earlier, logically entails that (**X**), "If *P*, then *Q*."

Here is an example of two steps of transposition, one after the other:

If a fire is burning, then oxygen is present.

(transposition) ↓ *(formally deductively valid)*

If oxygen is not present, then a fire is not burning.

(transposition) ↓ *(formally deductively valid)*

If a fire is burning, then oxygen is present.

Two steps of transposition carry us back to the original conditional from which the reasoning started. (Here we are merely moving back and forth between equivalent conditional statements, to illustrate their equivalence).

Transposition remains deductively valid when the antecedent or consequent of the conditional contains negative terms. For instance, given

If not *P*, then *Q*.

transposition yields

If not *Q*, then not (not *P*).

Since "not (not *P*)" is equivalent to "*P*," this can be reduced to

If not *Q*, then *P*

which also follows with deductive validity from the original conditional by transposition. Here is a concrete example of such reasoning:

If the electricity is off, then the lights will
not come on when you throw the switch.

(transposition) ↓ *(formally deductively valid)*

If the lights will come on when you throw
the switch, then the electricity is not off.

Much reasoning involves transposition, so be ready for it. Be certain to remember *both* to negate *and* to exchange the positions of the antecedent and consequent clauses — otherwise the deductive validity of the inference is not guaranteed by its form.

It is important *NOT* to confuse the transpositive form of a conditional with its "converse." The converse of "If *X*, then *Y*" is "If *Y*, then *X*." To replace a conditional with its converse is NOT automatically valid. That is, the truth of a conditional DOES NOT automatically imply the truth of its converse form. This does not mean, of course, that if a conditional is true, then its converse is false, but only that it *can* happen that a conditional is true and yet its converse form be false. (For example, "If a fire is burning, then oxygen is present" is true, but its converse, "If oxygen is present, then a fire is burning" is not always true.) So, from a conditional statement alone, one cannot automatically infer that its converse is true.

The philosopher John Locke appears to make this mistake in a passage of his essay, "Of Property," that can be abridged as follows:

> The materials of nature (air, earth, water) that remain untouched by
> human effort belong to no one and are not property. It follows that a
> thing can become someone's private property only if he works and labors
> on it to change its natural state. From this I conclude that whatever a
> man improves by the labor of his hand and brain belongs to him, and to
> him only.

The basic structure of this reasoning can be outlined as follows:

1. If not worked-on, then not property.

(deductively valid)

2. Property only if worked on.

(invalid)

3. If worked on, then property.

Locke's step from 1 to 2 is deductively valid. It combines transposition with a transformation of the conditional from its "If . . ., then _ _ _ " form to its ". . . only if _ _ _ " form — that is, from its "If *P*, then *Q*" form to its "*P* only if *Q*" form.

To clarify this, the step from 1 to 2 can be separated into two steps as follows:

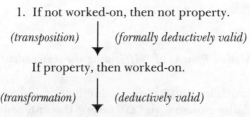

1. If not worked-on, then not property.

(transposition)   *(formally deductively valid)*

If property, then worked-on.

(transformation)   *(deductively valid)*

2. Property only if worked-on.

But Locke's next step is fallacious. From conditional (2) he invalidly infers its converse, and the labor that began as merely a necessary condition of property ownership suddenly is invalidly inferred to be a sufficient condition:

2. Property only if worked-on.

(invalid)

3. If worked-on then property.

This step of inference is invalid because statement 2 only says that in order for something to be someone's property, that person must have worked on it. In other words, it says that something is not mine unless I have worked on it, and it is not yours unless you have worked on it.

Since this is only given as a necessary condition for ownership, it does not say or logically imply that merely working on something is enough (that is, sufficient) to make it yours or mine. Statement 2 does not logically imply that if I go over to your place to help you work on your house or car, then it belongs to me. But this is the conclusion invalidly drawn in statement 3. Statement 3 logically implies, for example, that if you worked on someone else's house or car, then it would automatically be your property, a conclusion that does not follow logically from statement 2.

Locke's fallacious reasoning has the following invalid form:

P only if W.

(invalid)

If W, then P.

Did you detect this fallacy in Locke's reasoning when you originally read the passage, or did you see it only when the reasoning was subjected to careful logical evaluation?

Modus Ponens or "Affirming the Antecedent"

Another important pattern of deductively valid inference involving conditionals is "**modus ponens**" or "**affirming the antecedent**." It is another inference whose validity is due entirely to its logical form. Its form looks like this:

$$\frac{P \quad + \quad \text{If P, then Q.}}{}$$

(*modus ponens*)   ↓   (*formally deductively valid*)

Q.

The rule of inference of "affirming the antecedent" or "modus ponens" can be stated in words as follows:

MODUS PONENS: Given the statement of a conditional plus a statement that its antecedent is true, infer that its consequent is true.

The deductive validity of modus ponens is an obvious consequence of the meaning of conditional statements. For, any statement of the form "*If* ANTECEDENT *then* CONSEQUENT" implies that in case the antecedent clause is true, so also is the consequent clause. In reasoning that uses modus ponens, the additional premise states that the antecedent *is* true; therefore, from the combination of the two premises, it follows logically that the consequent is true. This step of reasoning is also called "affirming the antecedent," because one premise affirms the truth of the antecedent of the conditional that is the other premise.

Notice that the *order* in which the two premises come in the diagram does *not* matter, and that the antecedent that is affirmed (and the consequent that is inferred) can be stated in either positive or negative form. (The same was true of transposition earlier) Thus, the following example also represents an instance of modus ponens:

$$\frac{\text{If not R, then not J.} \quad + \quad \text{Not R.}}{}$$

(*modus ponens*)   ↓   (*formally deductively valid*)

Not J.

Here the premise "Not R" affirms the truth of the antecedent of the conditional, from which the consequent "Not J" is validly inferred.

Modus ponens occurs in the song that the famous storybook character, Winnie the Pooh, sang while sitting midstream on a warm rock in the sunshine:[1]

> *I could spend a happy morning*
> *Seeing Roo,*
> *I could spend a happy morning*
> *Being Pooh,*
> *For it doesn't seem to matter,*
> *If I* don't *get any fatter*
> *(And I* don't *get any fatter)*
> *What I do.*

Pooh's reasoning can be diagrammed as follows:

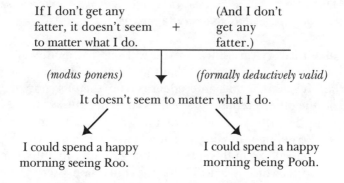

As mentioned, modus ponens is also called "affirming the antecedent." Pooh Bear affirms his antecedent (doing it in parentheses) right in the middle of stating his conditional.[2] Incidentally, the bottom two arrows in the diagram show what is called a "divergent inference," in which two different conclusions are drawn from the same one intermediate conclusion (the statement that "It doesn't

---

[2]And to think that Eeyore always maintained that Pooh had only fluff in his head!

seem to matter what I do").

Modus Tollens or "Denying the Consequent"

Another pattern of inference that is deductively valid simply because of its logical form is called "**modus tollens**" or "**denying the consequent**." In outline form, it looks like this:

If P, then Q. + Not Q.
_____

(modus tollens)   ↓   *(formally deductively valid)*

Not P.

This deductively valid pattern of inference can be expressed in words in the form of a rule of inference as follows:

MODUS TOLLENS: *Given the statement of a conditional plus a statement that its consequent is not true, infer that its antecedent is not true.*

Think about it very carefully and you will see that modus tollens is also always deductively valid. For suppose that the conditional statement given as a premise is true. It says that if its antecedent is true, then its consequent also is true. However, the other premise says that its consequent is *not* true. From this we can conclude that the antecedent of this conditional is not true either, because if it were true, then its consequent would be true too, which the other premise has just denied. So in this situation, one can infer that this conditional's antecedent is not true, which is exactly what the conclusion asserts.

Modus tollens leads to the same conclusion as would a step of transposition followed by a step of modus ponens:

If P, then Q.

(transposition)   ↓   *(formally deductively valid)*

If not Q, then not P. + Not Q.

(modus ponens)   ↓   *(formally deductively valid)*

Not P.

Since modus tollens leads to the same conclusion as the combination of these other deductively valid steps of reasoning, modus tollens is also deductively valid.

The reasoning in the following quotation employs modus tollens, for example, as well as a pure hypothetical syllogism. (Two conditional statements are hidden in this passage. Can you find them as you read it?) Here "probable" means "likely," while "empirical" and "experimental" mean "testable by observation."

> What is not so generally recognized is that there can be no way of proving that the existence of a god, such as the God of Christianity, is even probable. Yet this also is easily shown. For if the existence of such a god were probable, then the proposition that he existed would be an empirical hypothesis. And in that case it would be possible to deduce from it, and other empirical hypotheses, certain experiential propositions which were not deducible from those other hypotheses alone. But in fact this is not possible.
>
> From A. J. Ayer, *Language, Truth and Logic* (New York: Dover, 1952), p. 115. (Cited by Pospesel.)

The reasoning in this passage can be diagrammed as follows:

If the existence of a god, such as the God of Christianity, were probable, then the proposition that he existed would be an empirical hypothesis.	+	If the proposition that God exists were an empirical hypothesis, then it would be possible to deduce from it, and other empirical hypotheses, certain experiential propositions which were not deducible from those other hypotheses alone.

(pure hypothetical syllogism)   *(formally deductively valid)*

[If the existence of a god, such as the God of Christianity, were probable, then it would be possible to deduce from the proposition that he exists and other empirical hypotheses, certain experiential propositions which were not deducible from those other hypotheses alone.]	+	This is not possible.

(modus tollens)   *(formally deductively valid)*

[The existence of a god, such as the God of Christianity, is not probable.]

The general abstract form of this reasoning is:

If P, then Q. + If Q, then R.
_____

(pure hypothetical syllogism) ↓ *(formally deductively valid)*

[If P, then R.] + Not R.
_____

(modus tollens) ↓ *(formally deductively valid)*

[Not P.]

This very important argument, then, is deductively valid. (Whether it is also sound depends on whether all three of its basic premises are true.)

Disjunctive Syllogism

The **"disjunctive syllogism"** (sometimes also loosely called "the either-or" pattern of inference) occurs when a premise of the form "Either P or Q" is combined with another premise that *denies* one of the given alternatives, and the conclusion is drawn that the other alternative must be true in that case. In outline form it looks like this:

Either R or S.   +   Not R.
_____

(disjunctive syllogism) ↓ *(formally deductively valid)*

S.

This form of inference remains deductively valid when the word "either" is omitted. Also, the other premise can deny either the first or the second of the two alternatives, or "disjuncts" as they are called. And like the other deductively valid forms previously explained, the reasoning also remains deductively valid when negated statements are substituted for each occurrence of a letter in the deductively valid outline form.

4. Unreliable Forms of Inference Involving Conditionals

Two invalid, or fallacious, patterns of inference sometimes masquerade as valid forms, and must be guarded against. One is called "the fallacy of affirming the consequent." In outline, it looks like this:

FALLACY OF AFFIRMING THE CONSEQUENT

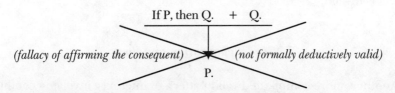

I have crossed it out to emphasize that it is not a valid form. Here is an example in which reasoning of this invalid form leads from truths to a falsehood:

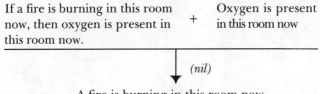

The conditional on the top left is true, and oxygen is present in my room now, but no fire is burning. So, unlike modus ponens and modus tollens, arguments having the crossed-out form are not guaranteed to be reliable.

Another imposter to guard against is "the fallacy of denying the antecedent."

FALLACY OF DENYING THE ANTECEDENT

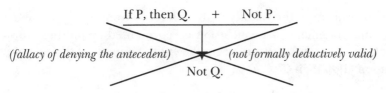

Here is an example in which reasoning of this deceptive form leads from truths to a falsehood:

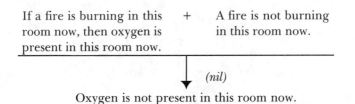

This conclusion can obviously be false when the premises are true, so this reasoning is invalid.

5. *Conditionalization and Boxes*

Another, more complicated valid pattern of inference involving conditional statements, called **"conditionalization,"** goes as follows. *Suppose* that it would be deductively valid to reason from some assumption, *A*, to conclusion, *C*, like this:

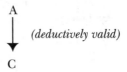

If this reasoning is deductively valid, this means that if assumption *A* be true, then conclusion *C* is also true (simply by the definition of deductive validity together with the deductive validity of the reasoning).

So, simply from the validity of the step of reasoning, one can infer the *truth* of a *conditional statement* whose antecedent is the same as assumption *A*, and whose consequent is the same as the inferred conclusion *C* — that is, from the validity of the above inference one can validly conclude:

If *A*, then *C*.

Reasoning like this from the validity of the inference from *A* to *C* to the truth of the conditional statement as a conclusion is represented by putting the step of reasoning from *A* to *C* in a *box* and using the entire contents of this box to justify the conclusion "If *A*, then *C*":

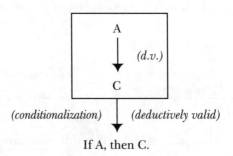

If A, then C.

A box is used here because, in this reasoning, it is neither statement A, nor statement C, that justifies the conditional drawn as a conclusion; rather this conditional is justified by the validity of the step of inference from A to C. Here is an extremely simple illustration:

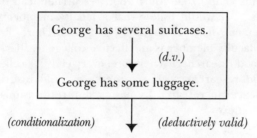

(*conditionalization*)   (*deductively valid*)

If George has several suitcases, then George has some luggage.

In diagramming steps of conditionalization like this, the top of the box is closed (that is, a horizontal line is drawn across the top of the box) to show that the truth of the conditional statement inferred as a conclusion does not depend on the truth of the statement assumed, or pictured as a basic reason or premise, inside the box. If the reasoning inside the box is deductively valid, then even if the statement, *A,* shown as a reason inside the box (for example, "George has several suitcases") happens to be false, the truth of the conditional statement, "If *A,* then *C,*" below the box (for example, "If George has several suitcases, then George has some luggage") still is guaranteed. The deductive validity of the reasoning inside the box, by itself, already guarantees the truth of the conditional statement concluded below the box.

Drawing a line across the top of the box expresses the fact that the assumption, *A,* below the top line in the box is "discharged." This means that the basic assumption, *A,* inside the box below the top line is NOT assumed as a basic reason or assumption in the justification for the conditional drawn as a conclusion. (Only the *validity* of the inference inside the box is assumed.) Putting reasoning inside a box and closing the box across the top means that every assumption inside the box below the line is "hypothetical" as far as the reasoning outside the box is concerned.

For instance, consider the following reasoning about the importance that teaching effectiveness should have in college faculty tenure decisions [1]:

---

[1]Adapted from Edgar Romero, "Tenure, Teaching, and Academic Freedom," *The Daily* (June, 1978), p. 10.

Suppose it were true, as some "publish or perish" proponents often claim, that "only good researchers can be effective college teachers." I personally do not agree with this statement, but suppose it were true (as my opponents claim) that "only good researchers can be effective college teachers." It would follow that a faculty member will be an effective teacher *only if* he or she is a good researcher. From this it follows that *if* a faculty member is an effective college teacher, *then* he or she must be a good researcher. Therefore, every effective college teacher must be a good researcher. If so, then we could insure that the university will excel in research by basing tenure decisions solely on teaching effectiveness.

This line of reasoning, which involves a step of conditionalization, is diagrammed as follows:

Only good researchers can be effective college teachers.
(d.v.)

A faculty member will be an effective teacher only if he or she is a good researcher.
(d.v.

If a faculty member is an effective college teacher, then he or she is a good researcher.
(d.v.)

Every effective college teacher is a good researcher.

(conditionalization)   *(deductively valid)*

If "only good researchers can be effective college teachers," then every effective college teacher is a good researcher.

If so, then we could insure that the university will excel in research by basing tenure decisions solely on teaching effectiveness.

The initial part of this reasoning is put into a box closed across the top to show that the author's reasoning and conclusions do not depend on the truth of the initial assumption that "only good researchers can be effective college teachers." (In fact, in the original passage, the author explicitly says that he disagrees with this statement.) The author merely *supposes* (or, if you like, "pretends" for a moment) that the claim in the box were true in order to show that *if* so, then it would logically lead to the conclusion that "every effective teacher is a good researcher."

(Do not make the mistake of rejecting an argument because it begins by assuming the opposite of what it is trying to prove. A proof that begins by assuming the opposite of what it is trying to prove can be sound.)

Next, after going through the reasoning in the box, the author performs a step of conditionalization, concluding that *IF* the basic assumption in the box were true, THEN the bottom final conclusion in the box would be true also: in other words, IF "only good researchers can be effective college teachers," THEN every effective college teacher is a good researcher. Notice that this *conditional statement* does not assume or claim that "Only good researchers can be effective college teachers." The conclusion drawn by conditionalization assumes only the *validity* of the steps of reasoning inside the box; it does not assume the truth of the basic reason (or any other statement) inside the box. This is shown by closing the top of the box with a line drawn across it.

Since every step of inference inside the box is deductively valid, the step of conditionalization is also deductively valid, and the intermediate conclusion "If 'only good researchers can be effective college teachers,' then every effective college teacher is a good researcher" reached by conditionalization has been proven true in a sound argument that depends on *no* basic premise.

Conditionalization arguments can also occur when some inferences inside the box are less than deductively valid. In such cases, the step of conditionalization itself will be less than *deductively valid,* but it can still be *valid* if the steps of inference inside the box are sufficiently strong.

Conditionalization also can be used when *more than one* basic assumption appears at the top of the reasoning in the box. For example, suppose that some conclusion C logically follows with deductive validity from the combination of several assumptions, $A_1, A_2, A_3, \ldots, A_N$. Using the letters '$U$', '$V$', '$W$', etc., to represent abstractly whatever intermediate conclusions are involved, such complex reasoning might look like this:

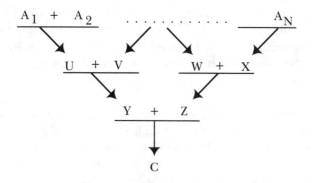

If every step of inference in this reasoning is deductively valid, then it follows logically that if *all* the assumptions are (or were) true, then the conclusion would be true too. That is, it follows logically that the following conditional is true:

If A_1 and A_2 and A_3 and . . . and A_N, then C.

So, the complex reasoning can be put inside a box and used to justify this conditional statement as a conclusion:

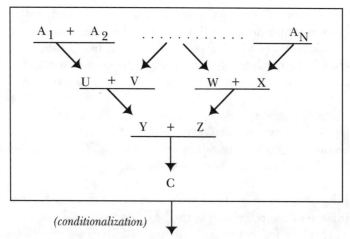

A variation on this pattern occurs when some statements that appear as basic assumptions in the reasoning inside the box are omitted from the list of assumptions shown in the antecedent of the conditional below the box. In that case, the top of the box is left OPEN above THESE statements (because *their truth is presupposed* by the reasoning for the conditional statement at the bottom).

In other words, when reasoning inside the box uses as premises further assumptions in addition to those that appear in the antecedent clause of the conditional statement below the box, the top of the box is open above these additional assumptions. Leaving open the top of the box above these basic assumptions expresses the fact that the last step of inference to the conditional statement below the box assumes that they are true.

Here is a concrete example:

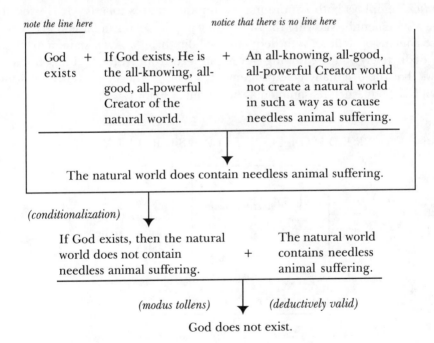

Notice that the top of the box is left open above the two assumptions, "If God exists, He is the all-knowing, all-good, all-powerful Creator of the natural world" and "An all-knowing, all-good, all-powerful Creator would not create a natural world in such a way as to cause needless animal suffering." It is left open above these assumptions because they are not repeated or included in the antecedent of the conditional "If God exists, then the natural world does not contain needless animal suffering." This means that the rest of this attempted disproof of God's existence depends on these two statements as basic reasons or premises. If either of these assumptions is false, the argument as a whole is unsound.

In conditionalization, the top of the box is closed with a horizontal line only above those basic assumptions that are repeated in the antecedent clause of the inferred conditional statement that appears below the box.

Reduction to Absurdity

A pattern of reasoning called "reduction to absurdity" or *"reductio ad absurdum"* employs both conditionalization and modus tollens. It is used to refute a statement by showing that it logically implies a known falsehood. When a false conclusion follows with deductive validity from a given statement, then since deductively valid reasoning never can lead from truths to a falsehood, it follows that the originally given statement is false. Where *"Q"* represents the known falsehood, such reasoning may be set out as follows:

REDUCTION TO ABSURDITY

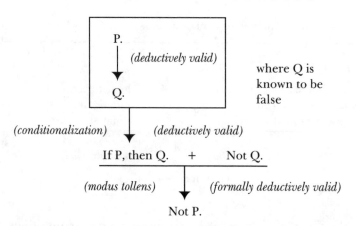

A discourse in which a reduction to absurdity occurs may have something like the following outline form:

Suppose that *P* were true. Then it would follow that *Q* is true. So, if *P* is true, then *Q* is true. But *Q* is not true. Therefore, it is not the case that *P* is true.

When people think to themselves in silent inner speech, and occasionally even aloud in informal conversations, reasoning involving conditionalization like this may be introduced by the phrase "If *P*, then it would follow that *Q*" instead of "Suppose that *P*, then it would follow that *Q*." On those rare occasions when the word "if" is used like this to do the job of the word "Suppose," then instead of being a conditional's consequent, the "then"-clause may express the conclusion of a step of reasoning that should (contrary to the usual treatment of ordinary conditional statements) be diagrammed with an arrow as the conclusion of a step of reasoning in a diagram in a box. (In diagramming most reasoning, however, what is in the "then"-clause should appear right after the antecedent clause on the same level in the diagram, and NOT down below it as if it were a conclusion drawn from the antecedent.)

Here is an example of reasoning that involves a reduction to absurdity:

Suppose (as some people have claimed) that the meaning of a word in a language were the same as the object or objects which that word names. Then it would follow that words (like "is," "the," "yes," and "nothing") that do not name anything have no meaning. But this is absurd. Words like "is," "the," "yes," and "nothing" that do not name anything nevertheless have a meaning. Therefore, it is not the case that the meaning of a word in a language is the same thing as the object or objects which that word names.

Here is a diagram of this reasoning.

```
┌─────────────────────────────────────────────────────────┐
│ The meaning of a word in a language is the same          │
│ thing as the object or objects which that word names.    │
│                    │     (d.v.)                           │
│                    ▼                                      │
│ Words (like "is," "the," "yes," and "nothing")           │
│ that do not name anything have no meaning.               │
└─────────────────────────────────────────────────────────┘
```

(conditionalization)   ↓   *(deductively valid)*

If the meaning of a word in a language is the   +   Words (like"is," "the," "yes,"
same thing as the object or objects which   and "nothing") that

Continued on next page

that word names, then words (like "is," "the," "yes," and "nothing") that do not name anything have no meaning.	+	do not name anything nevertheless have a meaning.

(modus tollens)   ↓   *(formally deductively valid)*

It is not the case that the meaning of a word in a language is the same thing as the object or objects which that word names.

Reduction to absurdity is frequently used in philosophic, scientific, and legal reasoning.

Proof by Contradiction

In a special case of *reductio ad absurdum* called "proof by contradiction," a statement is proven true by showing that its negation leads to a conclusion that is not merely false, but a logical contradiction. In the original discourse in which such reasoning occurs, a proof by contradiction often appears in something like the following outline form:

I wish to show that *R* is true. To do this, suppose that *R* is false. It would follow that *S*. But *S* is a contradiction. Therefore, *R* is true.

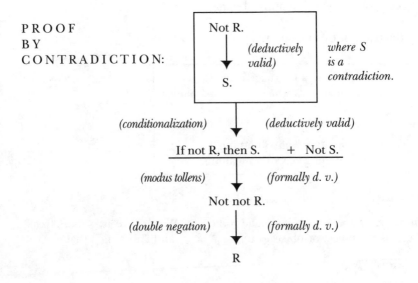

PROOF
BY
CONTRADICTION:

Not R.

↓   *(deductively valid)*

S.

where S is a contradiction.

(conditionalization)   ↓   *(deductively valid)*

If not R, then S.   +   Not S.

(modus tollens)   ↓   *(formally d. v.)*

Not not R.

(double negation)   ↓   *(formally d. v.)*

R

Proofs by contradiction usually occur only in mathematics, ethical reasoning, and philosophy. Obviously, of course, this pattern, like the previous ones, can also be used when some or all of the statements "S" and "R" are negations or denials of other statements, or stated in negative form.

Note: Some speakers apply the term "reduction to absurdity" only to proofs by contradiction. With such speakers, confusion sometimes can be avoided by speaking of "showing that the assumption logically entails a known falsehood" rather than using the phrase "reduction to absurdity" when speaking about arguments like the previous example.

The word "suppose" at the beginning of a passage of discourse very often functions to signal that the statement following it is a basic assumption in a closed-box subargument, and that this assumption will be "discharged" later.

Here is an example of a proof by contradiction, a famous mathematical proof that the square root of the number 2 is an irrational number (that is, that the square root of 2 cannot be expressed as a fraction p/q where p and q are whole numbers).

> Theorem: There is no rational number whose square is 2. Proof: Suppose the theorem is false, that is, that there are whole numbers p and q such that $(p/q)^2 = 2$. We may safely suppose that p and q are in lowest terms (have no common factors) since we can always reduce a fraction to lowest terms. If there are such numbers p and q, it will follow that $p^2 = 2q^2$, and hence p^2 is even. But if p^2 is even, p must be too. (to see that p, too, must be even, try supposing that p^2 is even while p is odd. If p is odd, then $p = 2r + 1$ for some whole number r; but then $p^2 = (2r + 1)^2$ or $4r^2 + 4r + 1$. This implies that p^2 is odd, contrary to our original supposition.) Consequently, q is odd since p and q were supposed to be in lowest terms. Now since p is even, $p = 2r$ for some whole number r and hence $p^2 = 4r^2$. Thus $4r^2 = 2q^2$, or $2r^2 = q^2$. But this implies that q^2 is even and hence, so is q. Thus q is both odd and even. This is a contradiction and therefore our original supposition must be false. In other words, there is no rational number, p/q, whose square is 2.[1]

The diagram of this argument on the next page shows a double nested conditionalization inside a third conditionalization argument. The basic reasons with no box closed over them are the actual assumptions of the proof. Notice

---

[1]Adapted from Courrant and Robbins by David Sherry.

how different boxes discharge — that is, close over — different assumptions in the proof. If you are not interested in the details of this quite complex, indirect argument, just try to locate the steps of conditionalization from the graphics, and then go on to the exercises.

Example of Proof by Contradiction that the Square Root of 2 is Irrational

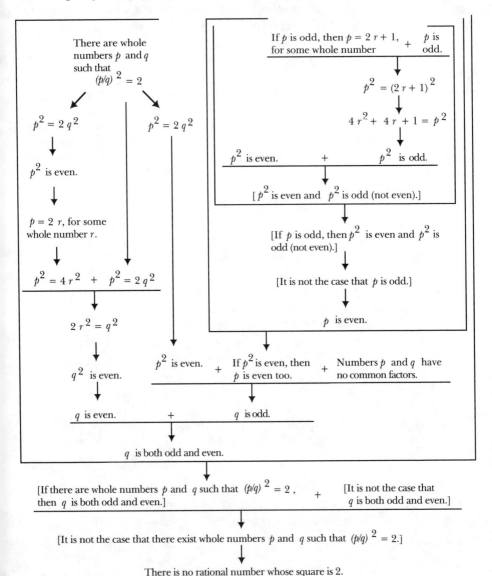

There are whole numbers p and q such that $(p/q)^2 = 2$

$p^2 = 2q^2$ $p^2 = 2q^2$

p^2 is even.

$p = 2r$, for some whole number r.

$p^2 = 4r^2$ + $p^2 = 2q^2$

$2r^2 = q^2$

q^2 is even.

q is even.   + q is odd.

If p is odd, then $p = 2r + 1$, for some whole number   + p is odd.

$p^2 = (2r + 1)^2$

$4r^2 + 4r + 1 = p^2$

p^2 is even.   + p^2 is odd.

[p^2 is even and p^2 is odd (not even).]

[If p is odd, then p^2 is even and p^2 is odd (not even).]

[It is not the case that p is odd.]

p is even.

p^2 is even. + If p^2 is even, then p is even too. + Numbers p and q have no common factors.

q is both odd and even.

[If there are whole numbers p and q such that $(p/q)^2 = 2$, then q is both odd and even.]   +   [It is not the case that q is both odd and even.]

[It is not the case that there exist whole numbers p and q such that $(p/q)^2 = 2$.]

There is no rational number whose square is 2.

EXERCISES 2A

For every step of inference in the following arguments, check to see whether or not it has one of the deductively valid forms explained in the preceding discussion of conditionals. If it does fit one of those valid forms, write "deductively valid." If it does not fit one of those valid forms, use the universal magic-question method learned previously to determine whether it is deductively valid in some other way. If so, write "deductively valid." If not, simply write "not deductively valid." (To save time on these exercises, you are not required to rate more precisely the degree of validity of the reasoning if it is not deductively valid, AND also you may SKIP the step of judging the truth or falsity of the reasons, and SKIP the step of giving a soundness verdict.)

Adapted from statements by George Meany, former President of the American Federation of Labor:

A-1. There is something basically wrong with our economy because a man working full-time can't support his family above the poverty level, and if a man working full-time can't support his family above the poverty level, then there is something basically wrong with our economy.

A man working full-time can't support his family above the poverty level.	+	If a man working full-time can't support his family above the poverty level, then there is something basically wrong with our economy.

There is something basically wrong with our economy.

Adapted from Henry Van Dyke:

A-2. Be glad of life because it gives you the chance to love and to work and to play and to look up at the stars, and if life gives you these opportunities, then you should be glad of life.

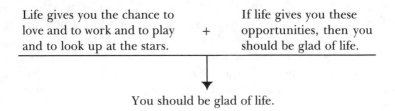

| Life gives you the chance to love and to work and to play and to look up at the stars. | + | If life gives you these opportunities, then you should be glad of life. |

You should be glad of life.

A-3. If this heater is tipped over, then it will not work. But it is not tipped over. Therefore, it will work.

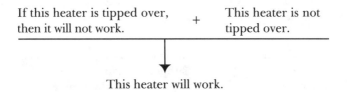

| If this heater is tipped over, then it will not work. | + | This heater is not tipped over. |

This heater will work.

A-4. You will be excused from handing in that homework assignment if you submitted a note giving an acceptable reason. You did not submit a note giving an acceptable reason. Therefore, you will not be excused from handing in that homework assignment.

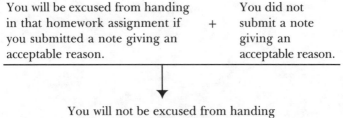

| You will be excused from handing in that homework assignment if you submitted a note giving an acceptable reason. | + | You did not submit a note giving an acceptable reason. |

You will not be excused from handing in that homework assignment.

A-5. You will be excused from handing in that homework assignment if and only if you submitted a note giving an acceptable reason. You did not submit a note giving an acceptable reason. Therefore, you will not be excused from handing in that homework assignment.

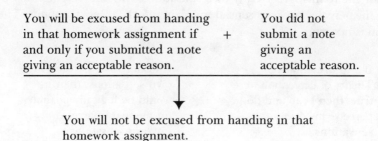

From G. E. Moore, *Some Main Problems of Philosophy* (London: George Allen and Unwin, Ltd., 1953), pp. 119-20. (Cited by Copi.)

A-7. I do know that this pencil exists; but I could not know this, if Hume's principles were true; therefore, Hume's principles . . . are false.

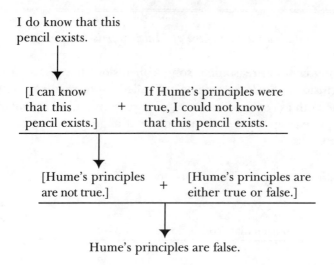

A-8. If a Representative Theory of Perception were true, then I can and do perceive my own sensations. And if I can and do perceive my own sensations, then it would be logically possible for me to misperceive my own sensations. So, if a Representative Theory of Perception were true, then it would be logically possible for me to misperceive my own sensations. But it is not logically possible for me to misperceive my own sensations. Therefore, a Representative Theory of Perception is not true.

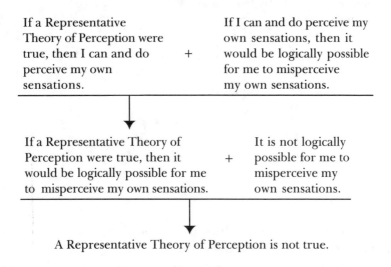

Analyzing the Structure of Multi-premise Arguments

In a long chain of reasoning, some conclusions may serve as reasons for further conclusions. Such statements are called **"intermediate conclusions."** They operate both as conclusions from prior reasons and as reasons for further conclusions. The diagram of such an argument might have the following form, for example:

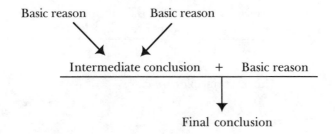

"Basic reasons" are those reasons that are not themselves supported by other reasons in the discourse. They are the ultimate ground or basis on which all the subsequent conclusions rest. Conclusions that are not used in the discourse to support further conclusions are called **"final conclusions."** They are what the reasoning attempts to justify or explain. Some reasoning may have more than one final conclusion. (The final conclusions are not necessarily the most important statements in the reasoning; they may or may not be the focal point.)

Making a diagram does not mean that one agrees with the reasoning. The diagram is only a picture made before going on to try to decide whether one agrees with the reasoning. We may or may not agree with it. We may even reject it after diagramming it.

Determining the Logical Structure of a Reasoned Discourse

After determining that a discourse contains reasoning and distinguishing the reasons from the conclusions, the next step is to determine its overall **structure.** In some reasoning the structure is obvious:

> Logic helps a person to predict the future, and deal with uncertainty,
> and make the best decisions. Therefore, it would be in my best interests
> to improve my logical skills. So, I should learn some logic

Here the pattern of reasoning is clear. It proceeds straightforwardly from a basic reason to an intermediate conclusion, and from that to a final conclusion. But in most reasoning the structure is less obvious. Sometimes inference-indicator words sometimes are left out. Sometimes they are present but the statements in the discourse appear in a confused or jumbled order. Various reasons for the same conclusion may be scattered about. A conclusion may precede its justification in one place and follow it in another. The author may make detours from the main argument. And so on. Such discourses require careful thinking before the structure of the reasoning can be determined. (In some cases, where the reasoning is especially complicated and the relationships unclear, there is room for reasonable disagreement about its actual structure.)

A long chain of reasoning may involve any of four different patterns at some point: SERIAL, DIVERGENT, LINKED, and CONVERGENT.

A. **Serial Reasoning.**   In serial reasoning, a single statement is both a conclusion from a reason and as a reason for a further conclusion — In other words, the reasoning proceeds via an "intermediate conclusion." The example about logic being in our best interests cited above is a serial argument. Using arrow notation, we can diagram it as follows:

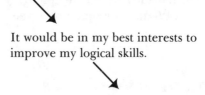

Logic helps a person to predict the future, and deal with uncertainty, and make the best decisions.

It would be in my best interests to improve my logical skills.

I should learn some logic.

Longer chains of serial reasoning are possible too, of course. The term "serial reasoning" also applies to the simple case in which a single arrow leads from one reason to one conclusion, with no intermediate conclusion.

B. **Divergent Reasoning.**   In a divergent inference, the same reason is used to support several different conclusions. For example:

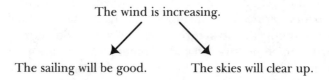

The wind is increasing.

The sailing will be good.   The skies will clear up.

A divergent argument can be treated also as two separate serial arguments (having the same basic reason but leading to different conclusions).[1]

C. **Linked Reasoning.**   When a step of reasoning involves the logical combination of two or more reasons, they are diagrammed as *linked*. For example:

---

[1] One also could join the two separate conclusions into a single compound sentence ("The skies will clear up and the sailing will be good") and represent the inference as a simple serial argument with the one compound sentence as a single conclusion. But for subsequent evaluation, it is usually best to leave them separated.

If marijuana were legalized,
then it could be commercially   +
processed and made available
in a form that did not need
to be smoked.

If marijuana could be commercially
processed and made available in a
form that did not need to be
smoked, then it could be made
safer for people's health.

$$\downarrow$$

If marijuana were legalized, then it
could be made safer for people's health.

Here the two reasons are connected by a plus sign, with a line drawn underneath linking both together. (Alternatively, if preferred, instead of '+', one can use the word "and" or the symbol '&', again drawing a horizontal line underneath to link the reasons together.) Notice that *a single arrow* is used to express the fact that the conclusion is drawn from combining both reasons together.

Reasoning is linked when it involves several reasons, each of which needs the other(s), or something like the other(s), to support the conclusion. In the preceding marijuana example, each reason needs the other in order to reach the conclusion. Linked reasoning with three or more combined reasons is also possible. *Deductively valid reasoning* involving the combination of more than one premise always is diagrammed as linked.

Reasoning that involves *statistical generalization* ("inductive reasoning") from several similar items of evidence or data *also* is diagrammed as linked. Consider, for example, the following reasoning:

I ate chocolate bar #1 and afterwards my face broke out. Likewise, for chocolate bars #2 through #N, each time after eating the chocolate bar, my face broke out. Therefore, I conclude that after eating a chocolate bar, my face will always break out.

Although each individual *confirmatory instance* (that is, each case of acne after eating a chocolate bar) by itself provides a little support for the conclusion, the strength of support is much greater when the instances are considered in union together, *and* each reason needs the truth of the others, or something like the other(s), in order for the conclusion to be supported.

Statistical generalizations are Linked Arguments

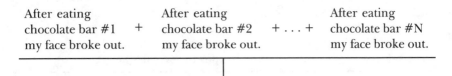

After eating
chocolate bar #1   +   chocolate bar #2   + . . . +   chocolate bar #N
my face broke out.   my face broke out.   my face broke out.

Always, after eating a chocolate bar my face breaks out.

This reasoning is properly diagrammed as linked, because if no outbreak followed eating a chocolate bar in some instances, the support given the conclusion by the other positive instances would be greatly reduced. Each reason needs the others, or something like the others, in order to support the conclusion.

D.   Convergent Reasoning. When two or more reasons do not support a conclusion in a united or combined way, but rather each reason supports the conclusion completely separately and independently of the other, the reasoning is convergent. For example:

I already promised Harry   If I go into the partnership
Schmedlap that I would go   with Harry, I probably will
into the partnership with him.   make a lot of money.

I should go into the partnership with Harry Schmedlap.

Neither of these reasons needs the other (nor anything like the other) in order for it to support the conclusion. Notice that more than one arrow is used to diagram convergent reasoning. A convergent argument is equivalent to separate arguments (or evidence coming from separate areas) for the same conclusion.

None of the discourses in the next group of exercises involves convergent reasoning, but be alert to its presence later.

Helpful Tips to Avoid Confusion and Mistakes

1. *Conditional ("if-then") sentences, in themselves (especially in printed discourses), are not instances of reasoning.* Sentences of the form "If X, then Y" (for example,

"If it gets warmer, then the snow will melt") are *not* instances of reasoning in themselves (although, together with other sentences, they may be *part* of an argument in the larger discourse in which they appear). The word "then" usually does *not* function as an inference indicator when the word "if" precedes it in the same sentence. By itself, an if-then sentence does not automatically imply that what is said in the then-clause follows logically, or is supported by, what is said in the if-clause. No step of reasoning is made when someone merely asserts an if-then sentence. Conditional sentences merely say that one thing depends on another. They do not say that one statement follows logically from the other. Conditional sentences are frequently confused with inferences.

Do not make the mistake of splitting the if-clause apart from the then-clause when diagramming. If you do, the diagram will not make sense or picture accurately the reasoning. This is important to remember because you will probably never get it to come out right if you make that mistake. For example, consider the following discourse:

> If I drive over the speed limit on Main Street, then I will almost
> certainly get a ticket, because Main Street is always patrolled.

When diagramming reasoning, do not confuse the words "if-then" with the inference-indicator words. The correct analysis of this reasoning is as follows:

> Main Street is always patrolled.
>
> ↘
>
> If I drive over the speed limit on Main Street,
> then I will almost certainly get a ticket.

The fact that the street is patrolled is the speaker's reason for asserting the entire *if-then* statement. He has not argued for or asserted what is in the *then*-clause of the conditional (that is, he has NOT claimed that he will almost certainly get a ticket), but only that *IF* he drives on Main Street over the speed limit, then he'll almost certainly get a ticket. Remember when diagramming DO NOT SPLIT APART AN *IF-THEN* STATEMENT!

Conditional statements usually only assert the existence of a connection or relationship of dependence between two events or situations. Although they often are important units or bricks in the structure of larger arguments, usually they do not constitute reasoning in themselves. (A few rare exceptions to this rule were mentioned earlier in the section on conditionalization.)

2. Here is one useful approach if you have difficulty diagramming the reasoning in the next exercises. Read the entire discourse through several times to familiarize yourself with it. Next, select an inference indicator word or phrase in the discourse that expresses a step of reasoning that you feel you more or less follow. Write down the conclusion of that step of inference, draw an arrow above it, and then try to write in more sentences from the discourse that the author evidently thinks support that conclusion.   If the reasons need to be linked together to lead to the drawn conclusion (as, for example, in the patterns of inference involving conditionals explained earlier), join them with a '+' symbol, draw a horizontal line underneath, and connect this line to the arrow pointing to the conclusion.   Be careful, as mentioned, not to commit the error of separating antecedent and consequent clauses that should stay together in conditional statements.

If you see that the conclusion does not follow validly from the reasons shown in your diagram , check to make certain that you have put the statements together correctly, and that you have not overlooked some other statement(s) elsewhere in the discourse that could be linked in to make a valid argument. If not, and you can see how someone might mistakenly think that the premises given do support the conclusion, then you probably have discovered a mistake in the author's thinking, and can leave the diagram as you made it.   But if someone else can arrange the same statements from the discourse together in a different diagram that constitutes a valid argument and agrees with all the inference indicator words present in the original discourse, then you did not produce the best possible analysis.

Next, if there is a second step of inference in the discourse, go to another inference indicator word and repeat the above process to diagram it.   If the conclusion of one inference is the same as a reason or premise of the other, add the new piece of diagram to the part of the diagram you produced previously. Continue in this way until the diagram contains an arrow for each inference indicator word or phrase in the discourse.

If someone points to an inference indicator word in the original discourse and asks which arrow corresponds to it, you should be able to point to an arrow in your diagram positioned above a complete sentence that expresses the same conclusion, with one or more complete sentences above it that say the same as the reasons given for that conclusion in the original discourse.

Of course, in situations where authors use extra, unnecessary indicator words (as, for example, when someone says, "Since *A*, therefore *B*," which uses the two indicators 'since' and 'therefore' to signal the single step of inference from reason *A* to conclusion *B)*, sometimes one arrow in a correct diagram will correspond to several different inference indicators in the original discourse.

EXERCISES 2B

Diagram each of the following reasoned discourses, using inference indicator words to locate each conclusion. Place above each conclusion the reason(s) given to justify it, and draw an arrow from the reason(s) to the conclusion. If the reasons need to be linked together to support the conclusion, join them in the diagram as shown for a linked inference. Then evaluate each step of inference (that is, each arrow) exactly as done in exercises 2A, as follows:

For every step of inference check to see whether or not it has one of the deductively valid forms explained in the preceding discussion of conditionals. If it does fit one of those valid forms, write "deductively valid" beside the arrow. If it does not fit one of those valid forms, use the universal magic-question method learned previously to determine whether it is deductively valid in some other way. If so, write "deductively valid." If not, simply write "not deductively valid." (On these exercises, you are not required to rate more precisely the degree of validity of reasoning that is not deductively valid, AND also you may SKIP the step of judging the truth or falsity of the reasons, and also SKIP the step of giving a soundness verdict, to save time.)

B-1. If the battery were dead, then the engine would not crank over at normal speed when I turn the key. But the engine does crank over at normal speed when I turn the key. Therefore, the battery is not dead.

B-2. If Bob did really mistreat Betty, then Betty would not want to get back together with Bob again. But Betty does want to get back together with Bob again. Therefore, Bob did not really mistreat Betty.

B-3. If there is static on your automobile radio that goes away if you turn on the headlights, then it is probably being caused by your voltage regulator, and there is static on your automobile radio that goes away if you turn on the headlights. Therefore, the static on your automobile radio is probably being caused by your voltage regulator.

B-4. This university will become an outstanding center for learning only if the State Legislature makes more money available to this university. Therefore, if the State Legislature makes more money available to this university, it will become an outstanding center for learning.

B-5. This university will become an outstanding center for learning only if the State Legislature makes more money available to this university. Therefore, if the State Legislature does not make more money available to this university, it will not become an outstanding center for learning.

B-6. If a person's soul is in proper order, then he or she will be ethical. So, if a person is not ethical, then his or her soul is not in proper order. But if a person's soul is not in proper order, then he or she will not be happy. Therefore, if a person is not ethical, then he or she will not be happy.

B-7. If there were no dust in the Earth's atmosphere, there would be no rainfall, because raindrops can only begin their formation initially by moisture condensing on dust particles. And if there were no rainfall, there would be no human life on earth. Therefore, if there were no dust in the Earth's atmosphere, there would be no human life on Earth. The presence of dust in the Earth's atmosphere, therefore, is a necessary condition for the existence of human life on Earth.

3

Evaluating Linked Arguments

Complex reasoning often contains multiple steps of reasoning in which many reasons are combined together to lead to several conclusions. In this chapter, we will learn how to evaluate fully the soundness of inferences in which several reasons are linked together to reach a conclusion. Next, we will learn how to evaluate fully the soundness of long chains of reasoning containing many steps of inference one after another.

1. How to Evaluate the Soundness of Inferences in which Several Reasons are Combined Together

Often, several reasons are combined to support a conclusion. Here is a general schematic picture of such a step of reasoning:

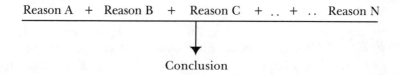

As always, in order to prove or explain its conclusion, such reasoning must meet the two requirements already explained in Chapter 1: (1) All relevant reasons must be true, and (2) the conclusion must follow validly from these reasons. After evaluating how well these two separate requirements have been met, the same direct-logic table from Chapter 1 can be used to appraise the soundness of the reasoning .

There is no special problem about evaluating the degree of validity (or degree of confirmation) of an inference in which several reasons are linked together to support the conclusion. The same magic-question procedure learned previously works here too. Pretend, suppose, or mentally imagine, that all the

109

given reasons were true, and at the same time try to think of any imaginable way(s) in which the conclusion could be false even supposing all the reasons be true.

If the truth of the reasons would make the truth of the conclusion so likely that there is no conceivable or imaginable way in which, if all the reasons were true, the conclusion still could be false, then categorize the step of inference from those reasons to that conclusion as *deductively valid*. If there are possible ways in which the conclusion could still be false even supposing all the given reasons were true, then estimate the likelihood or probability of the most likely of these possible ways. If the most likely of the possible ways in which the conclusion still could be false even if the reasons were all true is highly unlikely or improbable (such as, for example, an invasion by extra-terrestrials, or a sudden reversal of the law of gravity), then the degree of confirmation (or validity) of the step of inference rates as *strong*, and the step of reasoning still qualifies as *valid*.

But if some of these possible ways are circumstances of the sort that can and do happen in the real world (for example, a tire blowing out, or someone's telling a lie) then the inference rates as less than strong. If the truth of the reasons taken together would make the truth of the conclusion "a good bet," but not "a sure thing," then the degree of validity of the step of inference is *moderate*. On the other hand, if the truth of the reasons would provide some basis for expecting or believing the conclusion to be true but not enough support even to make it a good bet, then the inference rates as *weak*. Finally if the reasons taken together provide no support at all for the conclusion, then the degree of validity of the inference is *nil*.

This procedure for evaluating the degree of validity (or "degree of confirmation") of *linked* inferences differs from what you did on the simpler, nonlinked exercises in Chapter 1 only in the respect that *all the reasons together* must be taken into consideration when we imagine or suppose that the reasons are true. When using the magic-question method, for a moment imagine or suppose that *all* the reasons linked together immediately above the arrow are true. Imagine that all of them are true together, and then ask, in that case, how likely would be the truth of the statement given as the conclusion.

Before explaining how to deal with the second requirement (that all the reasons be true) in complex cases where we give different judgments about the truth or falsity of each of the linked reasons, it will be helpful to explain the concept of a "**logical conjunction**." A logical conjunction is the sentence that results from joining several simpler statements together with the word "and" (or any other equivalent grammatical conjunction) to form a bigger sentence that says that all of those shorter statements are true. For example, the logical conjunction of the statement "Bob is tall" with the statement "Ginger is slender" is the longer sentence: "Bob is tall and Ginger is slender."

The simple statements joined together in a logical conjunction are called the "**conjuncts.**" The *conjuncts* in "Bob is tall and Ginger is slender" are the two statements, *(i)* "Bob is tall" and *(ii)* "Ginger is slender." So, what was said in the preceding paragraph about "supposing or imagining that all the reasons are true together" also can be expressed by saying, "Consider the logical conjunction of all the given reasons and suppose, or imagine, that it is true." So, in other words, to evaluate the validity of inferences with more than one reason linked together immediately above the arrow, first suppose or imagine that the conjunction of all the given reasons is true, and then ask, in that case, how likely would be the truth of the conclusion, as just explained.

But the other crucial test in evaluating soundness (namely, judging the probable truth or falsity of the totality of reasons) is slightly more complicated when several reasons are linked together to support a conclusion. In order to prove or explain the conclusion, of course, all the reasons need to be true. If some reasons are true, while other reasons are false, then obviously, in that case, the reasons are not "all" true, so the step of inference fails to meet the requirement of having all true (relevant) reasons. If even just one relevant given reason is false, the inference fails to satisfy the requirement of having all true relevant reasons, and the correct verdict is that, because of this, the step of reasoning is unsound.

This rule can be expressed in our new terminology of a "logical conjunction of statements." In order for a logical conjunction of statements to be true, each of the *conjuncts* (that is, the individual shorter statements in the conjunction) needs to be true. For example, in order for the logical conjunction "Bob is tall and Ginger is slender" to be true, both the conjunct "Bob is tall" and also the conjunct "Ginger is slender" need to be true. If either of these statements is false, then the logical conjunction of them is false also.

So, as applied to reasoning involving the linked combination of several reasons, the requirement that all relevant reasons be true can be restated as follows: *In order for a step of reasoning to be sound, the logical conjunction of all the relevant reasons needs to be true.* Whether this conjunction is true or false, of course, depends on the truth or falsity of each of the separate individual conjuncts. If each and every linked reason is true, then the conjunction of them is true too. But if one (or more) of the reasons is false, then the whole logical conjunction of them is false. One false conjunct in a conjunction, like one bad apple in a barrel, spoils everything, so to speak.

Some additional useful terminology that will be useful here is the phrase "**truth value**," which gives us a concise way of talking about the truth or falsity of statements. If a statement is true, we will say that its truth-value is "true." For example, the statement "The sun is hot" has the truth value "true." And if a statement is false, then we will say that its truth value is "false." So, the truth value of "Unicorns exist" is "false." (The truth value "true" sometimes is mathematically represented by the number 1, and the truth value "false" sometimes is represented by the number 0.)

In order for a logical conjunction to have the truth value "true" as a whole, each of its conjuncts must have the truth value "true." So, for example, for the logical conjunction "Bob is tall and Ginger is slender" to have the truth value "true," the two conjuncts "Bob is tall" and "Ginger is slender" each must have the truth value "true." If either conjunct is false, then the truth value of the logical conjunction as a whole also is "false."

If we call the truth-value "true" a "*high rating*," and call "false" a "*low rating*," we can say that the truth-value of a whole conjunction is no higher than the lowest rating received by any of its conjuncts considered individually. The truth-value rating for the whole logical conjunction of premises is the one that should be used when employing the table to rate the soundness of a step of reasoning from the combination of these reasons to a conclusion. Since the truth-value of a conjunction is determined by the truth-values of each of its component conjuncts, one good place to start the evaluation of an inference is by circling each individual reason separately, and rating its truth-value by itself; next, circle the whole conjunction of these reasons, rate its truth-value, and use this rating for the whole conjunction to judge soundness with the table.

For instance, in the ridiculous example from Chapter 1 about dogs flying with their ears, the evaluation of the truth or falsity of the individual reasons was shown separately with two lassos:

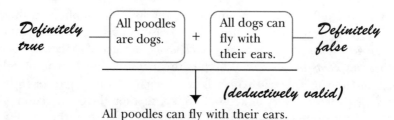

Definitely true — All poodles are dogs. + All dogs can fly with their ears. — *Definitely false*

(deductively valid)

All poodles can fly with their ears.

An overall soundness verdict is next reached by considering all the reasons together and rating the truth or falsity of their logical conjunction, and then using this value with the table. Since one conjunct is "definitely false," the logical conjunction is also rated as "Definitely false":

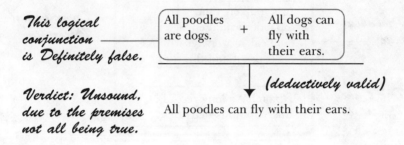

This logical conjunction is Definitely false.

All poodles are dogs. + All dogs can fly with their ears.

(deductively valid)

Verdict: Unsound, due to the premises not all being true.

All poodles can fly with their ears.

As shown in the table given in Chapter 1, putting the "definitely false" value for the conjunction of the reasons together with the "deductively valid" rating for the degree of validity yields an overall rating of "unsound."

The same principle (that the truth rating for the logical conjunction of the reasons is no higher than the lowest rating for any of the individual conjuncts considered separately) applies also when one or more of the conjoined reasons rate(s) as "Don't know/uncertain." "Don't know/Uncertain" can be considered on the direct-logic model to be lower than "true," but higher than "false." If I do not know whether one of the reasons in a linked inference is true or false, while I do know that all the *other* reasons are true, then the rating that I should give to the logical conjunction of all these reasons is the lowest of these ratings, which in this case would be "Don't know/uncertain."

This is because, obviously, if I do not know whether one of the conjuncts is true or false, but I do know that all the other conjuncts are definitely true, then I do not know whether the whole conjunction is true or false. If the unknown conjunct happened to be true, then the whole conjunction would be true, but if it happened to be false, then the whole conjunction would be false. The truth value of the whole logical conjunction in this situation will depend on the truth value of the conjunct whose truth value is unknown, and if I do not know its truth-value, then I do not know whether the whole conjunction is true or false. This situation arose for me in the Nixon example:

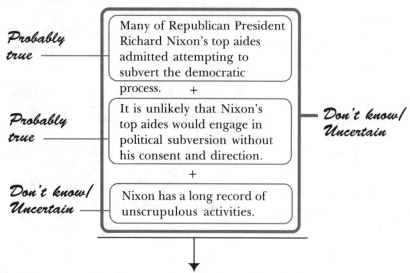

Probably true —

Probably true —

Don't know/ Uncertain —

Don't know/ Uncertain

Nixon was guilty of attempting to subvert the democratic process.

To save space, the small circles used to evaluate the individual conjuncts will henceforth be shown together in the same diagram with the large circle attached to its evaluation of the logical conjunction of all the reasons, even though, of course, the big circle is made and labeled after evaluating the individual statements enclosed in the smaller circles.

Since one of the conjuncts received the rating "Don't know/uncertain" and this is the lowest value for any of the conjuncts, the rating "Don't know/uncertain" for the conjoined reasons would be used with the table to evaluate the soundness of this reasoning. (Of course, someone else with more knowledge about Nixon's history might be able to give the truth-value of the unknown conjunct a more determinate rating, producing a different rating for the whole logical conjunction. The ratings in this illustration only show what little I personally know with certainty about the case.)

If we know that one or more of the reasons in a conjunction is *false* and we "Don't know" (or are uncertain) about some of the other reasons, then we know that the whole logical conjunction is *false,* due to the false conjunct(s) in it. Here again, the rating of the truth-value of the logical conjunction is no higher than the lowest rating received by any of its conjuncts—which, of course, is "false," when one or more of them is false.

Next, we need to consider the most difficult case: the situation in which several reasons rate as "Probably true" when considered individually and this is the lowest rating that any conjunct receives. Suppose that "Probably true" is the lowest rating given to any of the reasons, and that several of them receive this rating. What rating now should the larger conjunction of these reasons receive now? At first, one might think that, in this case, the whole conjunction also should be rated as "Probably true." This is indeed appropriate if there are only a *few* "probably true" conjuncts involved, but if the number of "probably true" reasons is more than a few (say, three or four), then it may be wise to consider lowering the rating for the conjunction as a whole below "Probably true" to "Don't know/uncertain" (or, in some cases, even to "Probably false"), depending on just how likely the truth of these reasons is.

This is because, as the number of "Probably true" reasons increases, the likelihood that at least one of them is false (and hence that the whole conjunction is false) also increases. Since logic attempts to safeguard against the possibility of error as much as possible, we must take into account the increased likelihood that the conjunction of these reasons may be false. This likelihood (that the *logical conjunction* of the "probably true" reasons is false) increases as the number of "probably true" conjuncts increases, because, at least so far as we know, each "probably true" reason has a small possibility of being false, and as the number of these small possibilities increases, they begin to pile up, increasing the probability of an error somewhere. Mathematical formulas can be used to calculate the amount of this increase in theory, but in most cases, the exact numerical values of the probabilities needed to use the formulas are not available, so in practice, one usually must judge the likelihood that the logical conjunction is true on the basis of a rough "rule of thumb."

To explain this idea initially, let us begin with a simple artificial example in which numerical values can be given (unlike the usual case). Suppose someone has fairly shuffled a normal deck of cards and prepares to cut the cards, and I make the prediction (or guess) that the cut card will *not* be the Queen of Hearts. I say nothing about what it will be, but only that it will *not* be the Queen of Hearts. If the chances of being the cut card are equal for each of the 52 cards, then in 51 of the 52 possible outcomes, I will be correct, and in one of the 52 possible outcomes, I will be incorrect. So the chances of my being correct are 51 out of 52, or 98%. If the cards are next reshuffled and again, before recutting them, I make the same prediction, the probability that I will be correct on the second cut is the same 98%. Now what is the probability that BOTH my first AND my second predictions will be true? The chances are slightly lower: to be precise, .98 times .98, or about 96%. As I continue to repeat the same prediction, shuffle, and cut, time after time, the probability that *at some point* the same guess will be erroneous gradually increases and the probability that the logical conjunction of all my predictions will be true gradually decreases.

Thus, as the conjunction of my predictions ("On the first cut, it will not be the Queen of Hearts, and on the second cut, it will not be the Queen of Hearts, and on the third cut, it will not be the Queen of Hearts, and so on . . .) gets longer and longer, the probability of an erroneous conjunct occurring somewhere, making the whole conjunction contain a false conjunct, and so be false, gets larger and larger. Therefore, the rating of the likely truth-value of the conjunction of all these statements gradually decreases as the number of individual conjuncts rated "probably true" increases. So too, in general, as the number of "probably true" individual conjuncts increases, the likelihood that all of them are true together decreases, since the likelihood that the whole conjunction contains a false conjunct somewhere, and hence is actually false, increases. The following evaluation of this example illustrates this principle:

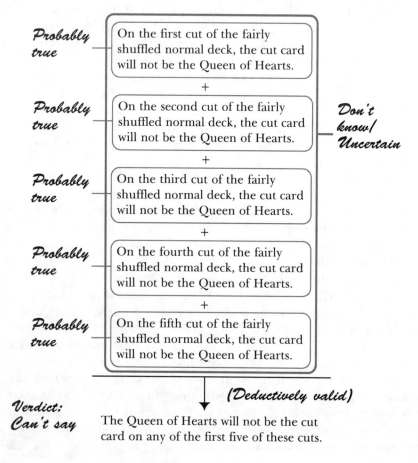

Probably true

On the first cut of the fairly shuffled normal deck, the cut card will not be the Queen of Hearts.

+

Probably true

On the second cut of the fairly shuffled normal deck, the cut card will not be the Queen of Hearts.

Don't know/ Uncertain

+

Probably true

On the third cut of the fairly shuffled normal deck, the cut card will not be the Queen of Hearts.

+

Probably true

On the fourth cut of the fairly shuffled normal deck, the cut card will not be the Queen of Hearts.

+

Probably true

On the fifth cut of the fairly shuffled normal deck, the cut card will not be the Queen of Hearts.

(Deductively valid)

Verdict: Can't say

The Queen of Hearts will not be the cut card on any of the first five of these cuts.

Each of these five reasons receives a "Probably true" rating, but the rating for the *logical conjunction* of all five decreases to "Don't know/uncertain" because the likelihood that the conjunction is false increases as the number of reasons rated as "Probably true" increases. In this example, "Don't know/uncertain" is the value that should be used in evaluating soundness with the table. So, since the inference is deductively valid, the verdict regarding its soundness is "Can't say" (rather than "Sound").

In a different case, if the probability that each separate conjunct is true were much higher, the conjunction of these separate statements could still be "Probably true." For example, if I buy ten tickets in a giant lottery, the whole conjunction

> My first ticket will not win, and my second ticket will not win, and my third ticket will not win, and . . . and my tenth ticket will not win.

is still at least "Probably true," because the likelihood of the truth of each individual conjunct is so extremely high. But in more ordinary cases, where the truth of the individual conjuncts is less likely, when the number of reasons rated "Probably true" goes beyond, say, about four, the rating for their logical conjunction should be dropped to "Don't know/uncertain" to be safe. If the reasoning is personally important, at this point, you should attempt to get additional information to enable you either to revise up to "Definitely true" (or perhaps, in some cases, downgrade to a lower value) your rating of some reasons previously rated as "Probably true." If this is impossible, at least you know that the reasoning is not absolutely reliable. Individual cases will vary, so you will need to use your best judgment cautiously.

Notice that, when carefully read, the same general principle given earlier for evaluating logical conjunctions still holds good: the truth rating for the logical conjunction of all the reasons is *no higher than* the lowest rating for any of the reasons considered individually. The words "no higher than" *leave it open* that the rating given to the logical conjunction *might be lower* than the lowest rating given to any of the conjuncts individually. And as just explained, in cases where the lowest ratings are many "Probably true" ratings, the overall rating for the conjunction of the totality of these reasons taken together often should be dropped to "Don't know/uncertain" (or lower).

Although many "Probably true" ratings may add up to a "Don't know/uncertain" rating for their logical conjunction, the conjunction of a lot of "Don't know/uncertain" ratings receives a "Don't know/uncertain" rating (even if some "Definitely true" or several "Probably true" ratings are mixed in with them). For, if you "Don't know" whether a statement is true or false, then, obviously, you cannot conclude from this that it is false, for it might be true. A lot of ignorance does not add up to knowledge. If I "Don't know" whether it is true or false, then I don't know which it is. *Knowing that a given statement is false* is equivalent to *knowing that another statement (its negation) is true,* and it would be amazing if one could gain such knowledge by adding more unknowns to a conjunction. Of course, if a conjunction of a lot of "Don't knows" also includes a known *falsehood*, then the whole conjunction rates as false, since even one false conjunct spoils a whole conjunction.

Evaluating Arguments Containing Many Steps of Inference

Important reasoning often contains many steps of inference. For example, a medium-length argument might have this outline form:

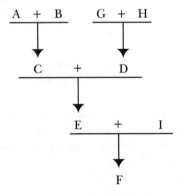

As you know, the reasons at the top of each branch in a diagram are called "basic reasons." In this example, the basic reasons are statements "*A*," "*B*," "*G*," "*H*," and "*I*." Reasoning containing several steps of inference is evaluated by determining the truth or falsity of the basic reasons, first individually and then collectively (in other words, the truth or falsity of their logical conjunction), and judging the degree of confirmation (degree of validity) of each of the steps of inference (represented by the arrows). The logical conjunction of all basic reasons may include conjuncts that were not immediately linked together in the reasoning.

For instance, in this example, statement "*A*" was directly linked with "*B*," and not with "*G*" or "*H*" or *I*," but the total logical conjunction that must be evaluated for truth or falsity is the logical conjunction of "*A*" with all the other basic reasons, including "*G*," "*H*," and "*I*" - that is, the conjunction:

$$A \text{ and } B \text{ and } G \text{ and } H \text{ and } I.$$

For the whole argument to be sound, this entire logical conjunction needs to be *true* (assuming that none of these reasons is extraneous). As before, the rating of the truth value of the whole conjunction is no higher than the highest rating given to any of the individual conjuncts. And again if the lowest rating of any conjunct is "Probably true," and if there are many of these, then the whole logical conjunction generally should be rated somewhat lower, due to the compounded effect of the many uncertainties combined together, as in the Queen of Hearts illustration.

The *validity* of complex reasoning containing several steps is evaluated by evaluating the validity of each step of reasoning individually, and then combining these evaluations. Each step of reasoning (represented by an arrow in the diagram) first is evaluated alone, in isolation from the rest of the reasoning, separating it, in effect, from the rest of the argument and considering only what is directly above and below this arrow. For example, in the current schematic illustration there are four arrows. The top left inference, for example, would be evaluated by evaluating the degree of support of the step of reasoning from reasons "*A* + *B*" to intermediate conclusion "*C*":

The other three inferences would be evaluated by considering separately each of the following three steps of reasoning:

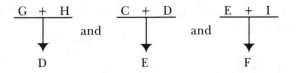

These one-step inferences are evaluated in the same way that one-step inferences were evaluated before. The earlier magic-question method for evaluating the validity of an inference with several reasons combined together can be used to evaluate each of these arrows separately. To evaluate the validity of each arrow, focus on the statements immediately above it, viewing them as reasons being given for the conclusion below it. It is usually unnecessary to bring in, or consider, statements that appear in other parts of the larger, total structure. For instance, in evaluating the step from "$E + I$" to "F," it is unnecessary to consider statements "A," "B," "G," "H," "C," and D."

Thus, this large complex argument diagram is broken down into a number of sub-arguments equal to the number of arrows in the diagram, and each sub-argument is then lifted out and evaluated individually, in isolation from others, as indicated by the gray triangles

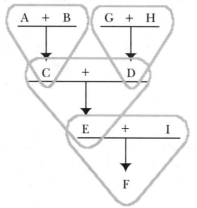

In the present schematic illustration, each of the four subarguments has been enclosed in one of the four gray triangles.

A rare exception to this procedure of completely separating the various steps of inference occurs when the degree of confirmation (validity) of a step of inference would be increased if other statement(s) from some other part of the diagram above it were added to the statements explicitly appearing right above that arrow. In such a case, one may insert the additional statements(s) at this second location in the diagram also. For example, if adding the statement "H" to "$C + D$" as an additional reason would increase the strength of the step of inference from "$C + D$" to conclusion E, then one may insert "H" in this second location also, and evaluate

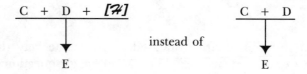

If other reasons had been given above "H" to support it, they should be added to the revised diagram above the second occurrence of "*H*" as well. All this is seldom required, however. Usually, nothing is gained by bringing a statement in the diagram down and recopying it in a second position like this, and steps of inference can be evaluated just as they stand, without doing so.

If each component step of inference in a long chain of reasoning is deductively valid, then the whole chain also is deductively valid. Or if the lowest rating of any step is "strong," and there are no more than two or three strong steps, then the degree of validity of the whole chain of reasoning also is strong. But if any step of inference is invalid (nil, weak, or moderate), then the whole chain of reasoning also is invalid. In general, the strength of the whole argument or chain of reasoning is *no greater than* its weakest step of inference. That is, the degree of validity of the whole structure is equal to, or lower than, the degree of validity of its weakest step. Here is a simple example:

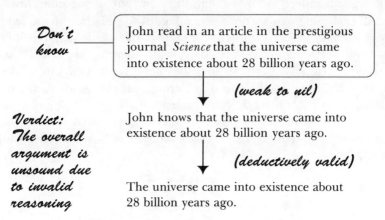

The bottom step of inference, going from the intermediate conclusion to the final conclusion is deductively valid, because the use of the word "know" semantically entails both that John believes it on the basis of adequate justification, and that what John believes is true. (If it be false that the universe came into existence 28 billion years[1] ago, then John does not "know" it, but only mistakenly believes it.) But the top step of inference, from the basic reason to the intermediate conclusion, rates "nil to weak," because someone's merely reading a claim in a prestigious magazine is not enough to establish that he *knows* it to be true. He may know that he read the claim there and this may be why he *believes* it to be true, but it is not enough to justify saying that he "*knows*" it to be true. Since the top step is weak to nil, the validity as a whole rates as

---

[1]The use of the figure of 28 billion years, rather than 19 billion, is intentional here.

"weak to nil," and hence the reasoning is unsound, despite the deductive validity of the bottom step.

Of course, there can occur situations in which someone starts from premises that really logically entail the final conclusion, but along the way, in a long argument, gets confused and makes some invalid inferences. This sometimes happens, for instance, when beginning geometry students start from the appropriate axioms and write at the bottom of their attempted proof the theorem they were supposed to deduce, a theorem that really follows from these axioms with deductive validity, but then show invalid steps of reasoning in between. Rather than quibble over whether such an attempted proof might nonetheless be called valid "in some sense" (since the theorem does really follow logically from the axioms), it is more useful simply to replace the defective intermediate portion of the attempted proof with valid steps of inference.

The most difficult case occurs when the lowest rating for any individual step is "*strong*" and there are more than three or four strong inferences in the total overall reasoning. In such cases (analogous to situations discussed earlier when there are a lot of "Probably true" reasons), the many small possibilities of error in the many "strong" steps combine to increase the likelihood that *somewhere* along the way, the reasoning has gone from truths to a falsehood. Consequently, if more than three or four "strong" inferences appear throughout the total diagram, then unless they are extremely strong, to be on the safe side, the degree of validity of the whole chain of reasoning usually should be rated lower than "strong" — either "Can't tell" or "moderate." At least, one should be cautious.

Salvaging Defective Reasoning

The most noble objective in evaluating reasoning is not to "refute" other people's arguments or to show that their thinking is unsound, but rather, to reach the truth through reasoning, thereby possibly increasing our knowledge and consequently our ability to achieve worthwhile goals. Accordingly, it is a wise policy not to discard complex reasoning automatically simply because it contains a part that is unsound, since it possibly can be salvaged in several ways.

Chapter 1 mentioned that invalid inferences sometimes can be converted to sound ones by adding further known truths to the reasons given in the original statement. With long chains of reasoning, another possibility arises: sometimes much of it, including its most important consequences, can be saved simply by removing, or surgically cutting out, bad top parts of the diagram. In the previous schematic illustration, for example, suppose that the step from "*A*

+ B" to "C" in the top left of the original version were the only unsound part of the argument, and that although this part could not be fixed up or made sound in any way, suppose that when we looked at intermediate conclusion "C," we realized that we can be confident that this statement, C, is "Definitely true" (or even "Probably true") just on its own, based on what we happen to know independently.[1]

In that case, one could simply delete everything above statement "C" in the diagram and end up with a sound piece of reasoning leading to all the same further conclusions. The improved version would look as shown in the next diagram. Notice that it is identical to the previous diagram with the part above "C" removed. If the valuable feature of this reasoning happened to be, for example, that it establishes the truth of "F," then the modified version would still perform this function. However, if the important feature of the original reasoning had been its claim in particular that statements "A" and "B" (together with "G" "H" and "I") led soundly to "F," then the trimmed version would not accomplish or show this.

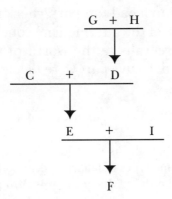

So, when a long chain of reasoning is unsound due to some fault in its top part(s), before discarding it, perform the test of evaluating the truth or falsity of the intermediate conclusion(s) that appear below the defective part(s). If you know that they are true, you can salvage the rest of the reasoning simply by cutting away the unsound top part(s). (Also, of course, there may be other applications for these sound parts, such as using them in other, *different* large arguments.)

---

[1] It should be remembered that the unsoundness of a step of reasoning does not mean that its conclusion is false; it only means that the reasoning fails to prove or explain this conclusion. Anyone confused on this point should turn back to Chapter 1 and review the discussion there around the example about "Wood is heavier than lead and therefore, most wood floats on water."

UNIVERSAL METHOD FOR EVALUATING LONG COMPLEX ARGUMENTS

i) Evaluate the truth or falsity of each basic reason individually, and then evaluate their logical conjunction.

ii) Evaluate the degree of validity of each step of inference. If there is more than one step of inference, go on to evaluate the overall degree of validity of the inference as a whole.

iii) Evaluate the soundness or reliability of the argument as a whole.

iv) If the reasoning involves more than one step of reasoning and is unsound due to a bad top part, check to see whether you know the truth value of the intermediate conclusions below those basic reasons, and reevaluate the worth of the argument that would remain if the defective part were deleted.

2. *Informal Fallacies to Avoid*

In logic, the term "fallacy" is used loosely to refer to reasoning that is defective in some way. Some types of fallacies recur so frequently that they have received special names, like the **"fallacy of appeal to authority,"** explained in Chapter 1.[1] Most common *"informal fallacies,"* as they are called, seldom appear in the theoretical writings of careful philosophers and other advanced thinkers, so we will not discuss them here, with two important exceptions: the *fallacy of equivocation* and the *fallacy of begging the question.*

The **fallacy of equivocation** occurs when one or more of the words, phrases, or other pieces of language in an argument has a double meaning and shifts between different meanings *in such a way as to make unsound reasoning appear to be sound.* For example, suppose someone were to argue as follows:

---

[1] Read Chapter 1, Example 2 (magnetic monopoles / *Physical Review*), and Example 3 (processed cheese / *New England Journal of Medicine*) again, if necessary, for review.

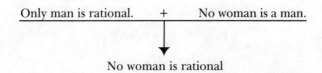

Only man is rational.   +   No woman is a man.

No woman is rational

Besides being sexist, this reasoning commits the fallacy of equivocation: In the course of the argument, the word "man" shifts meaning in a way that superficially makes the conclusion appear to follow logically, when actually the degree of validity is nil.

This "equivocation" happens as follows. In the sense in which we presumably understand the term "man" if we accept the first premise as true, it means the same as "mankind" and refers to human beings in general (as contrasted, for instance, with lower animals). In this sense, the top left premise really says something like, "Of all the animals, only human beings are rational." But in the occurrence of the word "man" in the second reason, where it contrasts with "woman," the word "man" evidently refers to gender and means "male." So the second reason really says "No woman is male." Between these reasons and the conclusion, the ambiguous word "man" changes from one of its meanings to another in such a way to make the reasoning appear sound when actually it is unsound.

A good way to detect and avoid fallacies of equivocation is by always keeping clear about the meanings of the words and phrases in what we read and hear. When a fallacy of equivocation occurs due to the double meaning of ambiguous words and phrases, it can be exposed by distinguishing and writing out all the different meanings. In the previous example where a fallacy of equivocation occurred due to the double meaning of "man," the two different meanings could be shown as follows:

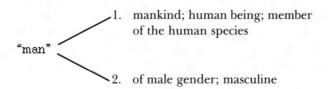

"man"
1. mankind; human being; member of the human species
2. of male gender; masculine

Once uncovered, fallacies of equivocation can be exposed by replacing the ambiguous language with *other* words that *clearly* express the different meanings that the equivocal language had in its various positions in the argument. In the example with the fallacious reasoning involving an equivocation on "man," the fallacy can be shown by rewriting the argument in the following way:

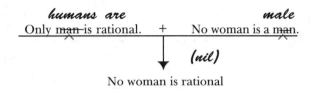

humans are
Only ~~man~~ is rational.   +   No woman is a ~~man~~.   *male*

↓   *(nil)*

No woman is rational

The unsoundness of the inference now becomes more obvious. Restated in terms that are not equivocal, it loses whatever appearance of soundness it improperly gained through the equivocation on the word "man."

Another flaw sometimes found in theoretical reasoning is the **fallacy of begging the question.** This defect occurs when, as one of its basic reasons, an argument depends on an assumption that is actually the same as the drawn conclusion. Such reasoning, which assumes the very claim that it is trying to prove, is said to "beg the question," be "circular," or to "argue in a circle." Here is a simple example:

> It is best to have government by the people
> because democracy is the best form of government.

In this argument, the reason given ("democracy is the best form of government") merely restates the conclusion ("It is best to have government by the people") in different words.

Reasoning can also beg the question in a less obvious way if one of its *unstated* or *hidden* assumptions is the same as the conclusion itself. Suppose, for example, someone reasoned as follows:

> It is clear that Jan likes me, for Jan said so
> and Jan would not lie to someone Jan likes.

This reasoning "begs the question," because the unstated hidden assumption behind the reasoning is "Jan likes me," which is the same as the conclusion. This can be shown clearly if we diagram the reasoning, putting the hidden assumption in square brackets:

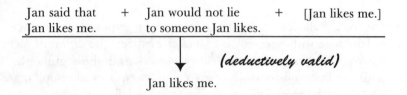

Jan said that   +   Jan would not lie   +   [Jan likes me.]
Jan likes me.   to someone Jan likes.

↓   *(deductively valid)*

Jan likes me.

Hidden assumptions are also called "suppressed premises." Notice that the "suppressed premise" needed to make this reasoning valid is the same as the conclusion, which means that this argument assumes the exact same statement that it is supposed to be justifying.

In more complicated cases of begging the question, the overall reasoning may look like this:

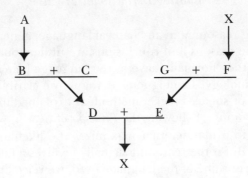

Here statement *X*, the final conclusion, is also assumed or presupposed as one of the basic reasons shown at the top right. It is easy to see in visual terms why such reasoning is called "circular"; one could draw an arrow of support from statement *X* in the conclusion to what it supports at the top of the diagram, and it would just go around in a circle.

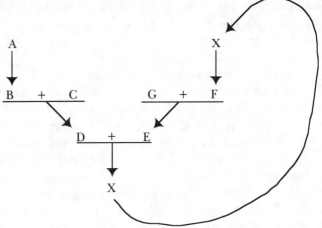

The same statement is ultimately supported by itself in this argument.

Reasoning that begs the question can be deductively valid and even sound, but it is defective because it fails to advance our knowledge. It ends up just where it started out. If we doubted the truth of the statement shown as the conclusion and needed some support for it, we would have the same problem or doubt about the truth of the identical statement as a basic assumption. When it fools people, deception is all it accomplishes.

Evaluating Definitional Premises

In evaluating reasoning in any natural language, generally the words and phrases used in the reasons and conclusions are understood to have the same sense or meaning they normally have in the language being used. And when some crucial terminology is ambiguous or vague, we clarify it, or pin it down, using the footnote or square bracket method, as explained in Chapter 1, before evaluating the reasoning. Following the *Principle of Charity,* we try to clarify any unclear language in a manner that maximizes the likelihood of making the reasoning sound. But if the reasoning actually involves a fatal equivocation on multiple meanings of some of the language used, we reject it as committing the fallacy of equivocation. All this we know already.

But what should be done when reasoning begins by introducing special *new* definitions or terminology? For example, suppose a mathematician begins a proof by saying something like "Let 'r' represent the length of the room . . . ," and then proceeds to reason algebraically from this, together with other assumptions, to some interesting, useful conclusion. Obviously it would be silly for someone to object to this proof on the grounds that "the symbol 'r' actually means something else." For the proof, it does not matter what symbol is used to denote the length of the room; any other term or letter could have been used instead to represent the length of the room.

This kind of definition is called a "stipulative definition." In the context of the mathematical proof, it can be taken as "true by definition" that the length of the room equals r. So, when judging the truth value of the assumptions in his proof, one can automatically write "Definitely true" by the circle around the statement presenting the definition that assigns this meaning to the term 'r'.

In general, statements giving stipulative definitions of terms used in arguments may be counted as true by definition automatically — assuming, of course, that no internal logical problem exists within the definition itself, and assuming that the same terms are not used with some different meaning elsewhere in the reasoning in a fallacious, equivocal manner.

Suppose, however, that someone uses an unusual, or even incorrect, definition of a term that *already has a different meaning* in the language we are using. How should one treat such a situation? The answer to this question depends on the context of the rest of the reasoning. If someone gives an inaccurate definition of a term that already has a different meaning in the language, and then proceeds to reason in a manner that equivocates fallaciously on the different meanings, we, of course, reject the reasoning as unsound.

As a simple example, consider the term "magnetic monopole," which in the language of physics normally is taken to refer to a magnet that has not two poles, as normal, but only one pole (for instance, a South pole but no North pole). Suppose someone tried to prove the existence of such fantastic objects by the following silly reasoning:

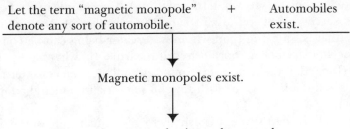

Such reasoning is defective because it equivocates between the normal meaning and the peculiar stipulated meaning of "magnetic monopole."

In evaluating such cases, it is risky to begin by straightaway rejecting the inaccurate definition of the term "magnetic monopole." Although doing this leads to no loss in this silly example, in general this procedure runs the risk of missing new discoveries and new knowledge, because important break-throughs often are presented in reasoning that uses old words in new ways. The sciences, for example, often give new meanings to words previously in use with older, different meanings in ordinary language (for instance, words like "element," "compound," "power," "force," "work," "valid," "sound," etc.) and express new knowledge with redefinitions of older words. In fact, advances may even involve redefining older *technical* terminology, as in the famous example of Einstein's rethinking of the concept of "simultaneity." Thus, it is sometimes rash to reject reasoning merely because it involves defining or using some term in a manner different from its usually meaning.

A safer procedure is to allow altered definitions of older terminology *tentatively* as long as they are clearly and explicitly noted, and then carefully check through the rest of the reasoning, watching for any equivocations, to determine whether the change in terminology leads to any important or useful new knowledge. That is, a safer policy generally is to treat any such definition tentatively as a stipulative definition of new terminology, giving a new meaning to an older term.

For instance, the philosopher Anselm gave an interesting, and controversial, famous attempted proof of the existence of God in which he began by defining "God" as "a being than whom no greater being can be conceived." Rather than immediately rejecting Anselm's attempted proof without examining it further simply because his definition of "God" differs from the definition we might give, a more reasonable and potentially more promising procedure would be tentatively to let Anselm use the term with this definition, and then look at his attempted proof to see what (if anything) it accomplishes. For if this philosopher succeeded in soundly proving the existence of a being fitting this description (that is, "a being than whom no greater being can be conceived"), this would be an extremely important result regardless of what name we gave to this being. (Indeed, if the proof were sound, we might even consider replacing our previous definition of "God" with Anselm's new definition and adopting his terminology.)

In general, the best strategy is usually to give "the benefit of the doubt" to most definitions used in reasoning, treating them as if they were stipulative definitions of new terminology, and then carefully checking out the reasoning to make sure that it avoids the fallacy of equivocation and determine whether it leads to any useful new insights or knowledge.

This procedure does, however, need to be tempered with the following caution: No special problem exists if someone introduces a verbal description that no existing thing satisfies, or talks about a property that no existing thing has. For example, if someone defines "unicorn" as "an animal that looks like a horse with a single horn in the middle of its forehead and has such-and-such magical properties," the fact that there exists nothing satisfying this description creates no special problem. There are lots of general descriptive terms in language that nothing satisfies (for example, "perpetual motion machine," "elf," etc.).

However, if someone introduces a proper name (called, in logic, a "singular term") in a way that smuggles in the assumption that there does exist something that this term names, when actually it does not (or possibly may not), the result can be fallacious reasoning. For example, suppose a student began a mathematical proof by saying, "Let a denote the largest even whole number." The problem here would be that there does not exist any largest even whole number (because for every even number, you can get a bigger even number by adding 2 to it). Thus the definition is not neutral, because it already smuggles in the (false) assumption that there exists a largest even number. From this false assumption one could reason with deductive validity to some conclusion that was in fact false (for example, that there also exists a largest odd number).

This error can be prevented as follows. Whenever someone introduces a term that is supposed to be the proper name of some particular thing whose existence is uncertain or in question, we can insist on adding a second "default" clause stipulating something else for this term to denote in the event that nothing exists satisfying the first clause of the definition. In the example of the term '*a*' introduced by the imagined reckless mathematics student, for instance, we can add a clause saying ". . . or $a = 0$ if there exists no greatest even number" (or we can pick out any other object that we know exists for the term to denote in the event that nothing exists satisfying the first clause of the definition). We then can check the proof to see whether it establishes that the thing named by the new term *satisfies the description in the initial first clause of the definition,* rather than the description in the default clause. In dealing with attempted philosophical proofs of the existence of God, including a default clause in definitions is especially important.

In the same way, if we were drawing up a Last Will and Testament, after having named who is to be "the executor of this will," it would be proper to add further clauses covering the possibility that the person originally named as the executor might be deceased at the time when the will needs to be executed. We should stipulate who will be the executor of the will in that event. Alternative or "default" references are also often crucial in business contracts, computer programs, statements of rules and laws, and other important uses of language. We should try to anticipate unforeseen eventualities as much as possible.

EXERCISES 3A

INSTRUCTIONS: In the following exercises, (a) judge the validity of the step (or steps) of inference, (b) indicate the state of your knowledge regarding the truth or falsity of the reasons, first each separately, and then all together as a logical conjunction, and (c) evaluate the soundness of the overall reasoning (give a "verdict"). Your answers may be presented in either of the two ways outlined in the instructions for the exercises at the end of Chapter 1, except, of course, that in these exercises, you will need first to express what you know about its truth or falsity of each reason separately (for example, "first reason is probably true, the second reason is definitely false, . . . , etc."), and then give a further appraisal of the whole conjunction of all the reasons taken together.

A-1. Loaning money to a friend involves risks, because people who loan money to a friend risk losing the money, and they also risk losing the friend, if there is a disagreement about repayment.

> People who loan money to a friend risk
> losing the money.
>
>   +
>
> They also risk losing the friend, if there is a
> disagreement about repayment.
> _____
>
>   ↓
>
> Loaning money to a friend involves risks.

From Douglass C. North and Roger L. Miller, *The Economics of Public Issues,* 2nd ed. (New York: Harper & Row, 1973):

A-2. Everyone knows that life is not a stable path to the promised land . . . . Fire can strike our houses. Accidents can destroy our cars. Robbery can leave us without valuable possessions. And many things can cause our premature deaths.

Hint: You may need to clarify some language.

Fire can strike our houses.

+

Accidents can destroy our cars.

+

Robbery can leave us without valuable possessions.

+

Many things can cause our premature deaths.

Life is not a stable path to the promised land.

A-3.   Fictional Characters behave according to the same psychological probabilities as real people. But the characters of fiction are found in exotic dilemmas that real people hardly encounter. Consequently, fiction provides us with the opportunity to ponder how people react in uncommon situations, and to [infer] moral lessons, psychological principles, and philosophical insights from their behavior.

Characters in fiction [sometimes] behave
in accordance with the same psychological
probabilities as real people.

+

In fiction, the characters are [sometimes] found
in exotic dilemmas that real people hardly
encounter.

Fiction [sometimes] provides us with the
opportunity to ponder how people [might]
react in uncommon situations, and to
[infer] moral lessons, psychological
principles, and philosophical insights
from their behavior.

From J. Victor Baldridge, *Sociology: A Critical Approach to Power, Conflict and Change,* 2nd ed. (New York: Macmillan, 1980). Used with permission of the publisher. (Cited by Hurley.)

A-4. Income measures the amount of money coming into a family in a given year; wealth, on the other hand, is a measure of the amount of money a family has managed to accumulate over a long period of time. [So,] while income is a fairly good measure of the year-by-year flow of money, wealth is a much better indicator of how money is passed down from generation to generation.

"Income" measures the amount of money coming into a family in a given year.

\+

"Wealth" is a measure of the amount of money a family has managed to accumulate over a longer period of time.

"Income" is a fairly good measure of the year-by-year flow of money, but wealth is a much better indicator of how money is passed down from generation to generation.

Removing Excess Verbiage When Analyzing Arguments

Even the best reasoned discourses often contain unnecessary words that are not part of the actual reasoning. When analyzing such discourses, this excess language should be omitted from the sentences when they are rewritten in the diagram. Sometimes the extra verbiage does no harm except to muddy things, but on other occasions, it can mislead to such an extent that the original reasoning is misevaluated. This is dangerous. Discourses in which additional sentences must be written and added to the diagram in order to represent accurately the intended argument are also a problem, but this is a more advanced topic. For the present, then, let us concentrate on trimming away unnecessary extra language.

As a simple example, suppose someone says: "I know that P, because Q." The indicator 'because' signals that Q is a reason, but what is the intended conclusion? Is the conclusion "I know that P" or just "P" alone? It could be either, of course, but in most cases when speakers use this form of words, their aim is proving the truth of P, and not proving that they know it. In such cases, the words "I know that . . ." should be omitted from the conclusion in the diagram:

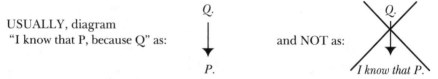

USUALLY, diagram
"I know that P, because Q" as:

$Q.$

↓

$P.$

and NOT as:

The words "I know that" in such situations usually are part of the inference indicator phrase rather than part of the conclusion. One exception would be an unusual case in which someone is trying to prove not only that P is true, but moreover that he or she *knows* this. In such rare cases, it would be appropriate to include the words "I know that" as part of the conclusion, and to require the argument to contain such additional premises as would justify not only P, but the further claim that the speaker "knows" that P. But generally, the conclusion is just "P."

Much wording found in reasoning is excess baggage that clouds and confuses. Simple, obvious examples are lengthy inference indicator phrases like ". . . as is clear to see from the fact that . . . ," "no informed person could fail to be convinced of this from that fact that . . . ," "from this it follows with undeniable certainty that . . . ," "the most important reason for this, which should always be born in mind, is ... ," etc. The "meat" or substance of the reasoning is usually in the clause that follows the word 'that' in such phrases. The rest is just fat. The meat of an argument is called its **"substance."** When diagramming, listening, or reading, go straight for the substance. Cut the fat.

EXERCISES 3B

INSTRUCTIONS: Each of the following arguments commits one or more of the three fallacies: appeal to authority, equivocation, or begging the question. On a separate sheet of paper, make a diagram of the substance of the argument, removing the extra words. Next, state which fallacy is (or which fallacies are) committed by each example. If the fallacy of equivocation is committed, tell which language is equivocated upon, and define its different meanings in the argument. If the argument does not commit one of the three fallacies listed above, write "This argument does not commit one of the three listed fallacies."

B-1. The Senator was mad about losing the election, and mad people ought to be institutionalized, so the Senator ought to be institutionalized.

B-2. Weapons and other aid should continue to be provided to US-supported right-wing military dictatorships in Latin American, because it would be wrong to cut off support for these conservative forces that the United States brought to power and supported in the past.

B-3. John left his money on the bank of the river when he went swimming and banks usually keep money in a secure place, so John's money must be in a secure place.

B-4. I know from experience that marijuana is neither dangerous nor addictive. The government says that marijuna is just as dangerous and addictive as cocaine. From this I can validly infer that cocaine is not dangerous or addictive.

Adapted from a Laurel and Hardy gag:
B-4. This salad is supposed to be served undressed, so you'd better remove your clothes before bringing it to the table.
Hint: Think again before omitting the "must" from the diagram for this one.

B-6. The United States CIA says that the charges that CIA sharpshooters with rifles firing from behind the grassy knoll actually assassinated President Kennedy, with Oswald up as a patsy, are too ridiculous to answer, and the CIA should know best whether or not it assassinated President Kennedy. Therefore, Kennedy was not assassinated by the CIA.

B-7. Enlisted men are often the superior of their military officers both in intelligence and physical ability. So, the idea that a military officer is the superior of his men is false. Therefore, officers must not, in fact, have any authority over their men in the military.

B-8 President Reagan said that he had no knowledge that members of his immediate staff were systematically breaking the law, and a U.S. President would not lie to the American people. Therefore, it is obvious that President Reagan had no knowledge that members of his immediate staff were breaking the law.

B-9. Our TX-10 Supertread road tire has unsurpassed traction. From this it follows with undeniable certitude that no other tire is better able to grip the road.

B-10. The County Commissioners will appropriate extra subsidies for the builders of the new stadium, and to say that an action is appropriate means that it is right and proper under the circumstances. Therefore, it is unquestionably true that the extra subsidies for the builders of the new stadium are right and proper under the circumstances.

B-11 We know that everything it says in the *Koran* is true, because in the *Koran*, it states that what it says there is true.
Note: The *Koran* is a book of Islamic scripture.
Hint: This argument contains two fallacies. What are they?

B-12. I know that it was the instructor's fault that my name was removed from the class roll sheet accidentally, because the lady in the registrars office said that it was the instructor's fault, and she ought to know. So, that's that!

B-13. St. Anselm's argument does not succeed in proving the existence of God, because St. Anselm gives no absolute proof in his attempted demonstration of the existence of God.

B-14. The Food and Drug Administration (FDA) says that taking vitamin C has no effectiveness against the common cold, and the FDA is a branch of the U.S. government. So, no informed person could fail to be convinced by this pronouncement that vitamin C is not effective against the common cold.

B-15. This insecticide must be safe for use on fruits and vegetables intended for human consumption, as is clear for all to see from the fact that it says on the package label that it is safe for such use.

B-16 The proof that the paradoxes of religion and mysticism cannot be resolved is the fact that these paradoxes are irresolvable.

SUMMARY OF DEFINITIONS OF BASIC TERMS

Valid reasoning: Reasoning in which the reasons, if they were true, really would justify believing or expecting the conclusion to be true. In valid reasoning, the truth of the statement(s) given as the reason(s) (supposing they were true) would guarantee, or make extremely likely, the truth of the conclusion.

Invalid reasoning: Reasoning in which the reasons, even assuming or supposing they were true, still would not justify believing or expecting the conclusion to be true.

Sound reasoning: Reasoning in which the steps of reasoning are valid and all relevant reasons are true.

Unsound reasoning: Reasoning in which either one (or more) of the relevant reasons is false, or the step of inference is invalid, or both.

DEGREES OF VALIDITY

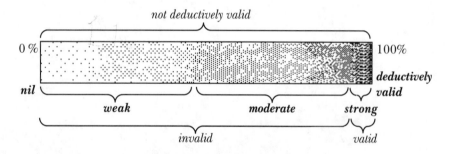

Summary of Degrees of Validity
(or "Degrees of Confirmation")

Deductively valid: There is no conceivable or imaginable way in which the reason(s) could be true and yet the conclusion be false. Truth of the premise(s) would totally guarantee the truth of the conclusion. It is logically impossible for the reason(s) to be true and the conclusion false.

Strong: If the reasons were true, they would make the truth of the conclusion extremely likely, certain beyond any reasonable doubt, "virtually a sure thing," but not totally guaranteed. (How likely is "extremely likely"? Likely enough to make it reasonable to stake something of great value on the truth of the conclusion if the reasons are true and likely enough to serve as a definitely reliable basis for actions.)